Portrait by Per Krafft, from Photographic Archives of the National Museum, Warsaw.

IGNACY KRASICKI

TWAYNE'S WORLD AUTHORS SERIES

A Survey of the World's Literature

Sylvia E. Bowman, Indiana University

GENERAL EDITOR

POLAND

Adam Gillon, State University of New York College
at New Paltz
Ludwik Krzyzanowski, New York University

EDITORS

Ignacy Krasicki

(TWAS 78)

TWAYNE'S WORLD AUTHORS SERIES (TWAS)

The purpose of TWAS is to survey the major writers —novelists, dramatists, historians, poets, philosophers, and critics—of the nations of the world. Among the national literatures covered are those of Australia, Canada, China, Eastern Europe, France, Germany, Greece, India, Italy, Japan, Latin America, New Zealand, Poland, Russia, Scandinavia, Spain, and the African nations, as well as Hebrew, Yiddish, and Latin Classical literatures. This survey is complemented by Twayne's United States Authors Series and English Authors Series.

The intent of each volume in these series is to present a critical-analytical study of the works of the writer; to include biographical and historical material that may be necessary for understanding, appreciation, and critical appraisal of the writer; and to present all material in clear, concise English—but not to vitiate the scholarly content of the work by doing so.

Ignacy Krasicki

By DAVID J. WELSH

University of Michigan

Twayne Publishers, Inc.   ::   New York

His sly, polite, insinuating Style,
Could please at Court, and make *Augustus* smile.

Alexander Pope

Principibus placuisse viris non ultima laus est

Horace

Preface

IGNACY KRASICKI (1735–1801) was Poland's major eighteenth-century poet. However, he has not been as well served
by translators as Poland's other major poets, Jan Kochanowski
and Adam Mickiewicz. Very little of his poetry or prose has ever
been accessible in a language of Western Europe.

One of the aims of this study has been to remind admirers of
eighteenth-century literature that the great figures of that period
were not restricted to England or France. Familiar names from
the Age of Enlightenment will be encountered here, though my
intention is less to draw analogies and parallels than to provide
a context in which Krasicki's literary achievements can be placed.

Sections of Chapters 2 and 5 have already been published in
The Polish Review (New York), and I am grateful to its editor,
Professor Ludwik Krzyzanowski for the opportunity to reprint
them here.

It is with pleasure that I dedicate this study to Professor John
Mersereau Jr., friend and colleague.

DAVID J. WELSH

University of Michigan, Ann Arbor

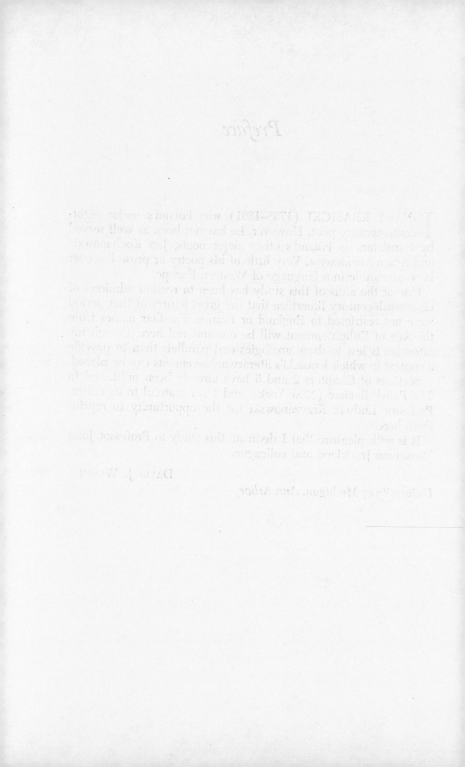

Contents

Contents

Chronology

1735   Ignacy Krasicki born February 3 at the Krasicki family estate at Dubiecko (Sanok, Southern Poland).

1743   Krasicki entered the Jesuit college in Lwów.

1751   Ordained into the priesthood.

1759   Krasicki completed his theological studies in Vienna and Rome (to 1761).

1764   Krasicki accepted an invitation from King Stanislas Augustus to edit and contribute to the *Polish Monitor*.

1766   Krasicki consecrated as Bishop of Warmia (formerly Ermland in East Prussia) and took up residence at the episcopal seat (Heilsberg, now Lidzbark Warmiński in north-east Poland).

1772   The first Partition of Poland between Russia, Prussia and Austria.

1775   Krasicki's most intensive period of literary creativity begins with *Myszeidos* (The Battle of Mice), *Mikołaja Doświadczyńskiego przypadki* (Adventures of Nicholas Find-Out, 1776), *Monachomachia* (The Battle of Monks, 1778) and its sequel, the satires (1779) and fables (1779).

1795   Krasicki consecrated Archbishop of Gniezno.

1801   Death of Krasicki March 14, in Berlin.

CHAPTER 1

Poland's Augustan Age

THE latter part of the eighteenth century in Poland was marked by a strong sense of literary identification with the writers of Classical antiquity, and more especially with those who wrote during the reign of the Emperor Augustus. Augustus (nephew of Julius Caesar) had shown himself to be the undisputed arbiter of Roman culture from the year 27 B.C. During the next forty years, Augustan Rome attained an unprecedented cultural dominance, thanks to the emergence of such remarkable and talented writers as: the poets Virgil, Horace, Ovid, Propertius, Tibullus and the historian Livy, among others.[1]

The election to the Polish throne of Stanislas Augustus Poniatowski in 1764 was auspicious, and the next thirty years were to constitute a genuine Age of Enlightenment and Reason, despite a series of political catastrophes which led to the downfall of the Republic. Needless to say, the parallels between Augustan Rome and Augustan Warsaw did not go unnoticed in Poland, any more than they had gone unnoticed by writers in London half a century before. To be sure, there were differences: the political triumphs of the Roman Augustus were not echoed by his Polish namesake. Politically, Stanislas Augustus was, to say the least, incompetent. However, his generous patronage of the arts, when he was in a position to afford it, was as well-directed as that of the Roman Emperor. Just as the Roman Augustus had patronized Horace and Virgil, and been eulogized by them with panegyrics, so King Stanislas favored his Court poets, who returned his favors in kind.

Yet Augustan Rome was above all a pagan society which persecuted Christians. How could the essentially Christian and Catholic society of Stanislas Augustus reconcile its faith with the secular paganism of ancient Rome? One reply to this puzzling question lies in the poetry of Horace, the Roman poet whose work was closest to enlightened eighteenth-century ideals, and the reasons for this are not hard to find. The urbanity of Horace, his restraint and sophisticated detachment, his distrust of sentiment, his realistic attitude towards the "facts of life," his clarity of utterance, and constant concern with metrical refinement and verbal dexterity— all these qualities appealed to eighteenth-century taste. Horace was also a moralist, and questions of practical morality interested writers and readers during this period. Society was entering a new stage of development, and people felt the need for establishing a new code of behavior: the manners and customs of earlier ages were found wanting, no longer adequate for more civilized minds. Horace was pre-eminently a poet of the Establishment, interested in values rather than in truths.

Hence, Horace's odes, satires and epistles were constantly studied by eighteenth-century poets, constantly imitated and translated. Twenty editions of Horace's poetry in English appeared in London between 1676 and 1794: in Poland, one of the most ambitious publishing undertakings during the reign of King Stanislas Augustus was the complete odes of Horace, translated by various hands (1773). The spirit of Horace is never far from any eighteenth-century poetry, be it English, French or Polish.

But there was a darker side to the picture. Warsaw in the late eighteenth century, like Imperial Rome under Augustus, was overcrowded and unsanitary, its inhabitants haunted by famine, beggars, mad dogs and outbreaks of plague. The splendid architecture of the royal palaces concealed the most primitive sanitary arrangements (as it did at Versailles or Schönbrunn). Wealth and gross extravagance were flaunted alongside wretched poverty. Sudden reversals of fortune descended upon the inhabitants of both Augustus' Rome and the Warsaw of King Stanislas. In both cities, poets and philosophers sought refuge from the corruption of the royal court by retreating into the countryside.

I   The Saxon Kings

The Augustan age of King Stanislas was long overdue in Poland. The seventeenth century had seen an almost unmitigated series of disasters—famines, Swedish and Russian invasions, and civil war. In literature, the "Baroque" period had produced original poets and prose writers since the 1600's, but a century later this style was decayed and debased.

The Saxon kings (1697–1763) ruled Poland mostly from Dresden, and played little part in the development of the lively arts, philosophy and the natural sciences that was occurring all over Western Europe at this time. Despite forward-looking efforts by such "great erudites" as Stanislas Konarski (1700–1773), Polish culture and her economy dwindled. Although the Polish-Lithuanian Commonwealth ranked as the third largest state in Europe in the mid-eighteenth century (after Russia and Sweden), its population was less than eleven million, and of these the Poles themselves formed only about half the total.[2] The remainder of the population was composed of White Russians, Lithuanians, Jews and others.

Education was reserved for the sons of the aristocracy and gentry, and was entirely in the hands of various monastic orders. The syllabus in these schools had remained practically unaltered since the sixteenth century, and was based on the memorization of an antiquated Latin grammar (Alvarez). The printing and publishing of books were also very largely in clerical hands. To be sure, some writers of the Golden Age of the Polish Renaissance were reprinted from time to time, but ninety percent of the productions of the clerical printing houses consisted of prayer-books, volumes of sermons, funeral orations, panegyrics, theological works and "calendars." The books themselves were clumsily designed with a square format, thick, badly-cut type and poor quality paper.[3]

However, signs of renewed cultural activities began appearing in the 1740's, when an increasing number of foreigners from the West started visiting Poland, bringing with them the seeds of enlightenment. They included a German, Mitzler de Kolof, who came to Poland in 1743 as tutor to the son of a wealthy magnate. Kolof took to publishing books and journals in Warsaw ten years later, and for much of his career as a printer and publisher he was associated with wealthy patrons, including King Stanislas himself.

Another German printer arrived in Warsaw in 1759: this was Michael Gröll, who opened a bookstore in what is now Theater Square. To mark his concern with what he thought the finest in Polish literature, Gröll adopted for his store the name "At the Sign of the Poets," thus demonstrating that he represented a new kind of book publisher in Poland. Instead of relying on patronage as Kolof did, Gröll was himself financially involved in the printing, publishing, sale and distribution of books. With his flair for knowing what the reading public wanted, Gröll was able to commission the writing of books and the translation of foreign works.

He was active in other directions too, importing recently-published books from Paris, London, Amsterdam and Berlin, and exporting Polish books. He issued catalogues, and held auctions to dispose of old stock. In 1769 he opened a reading room and circulating library, conducted an "information bureau," and even sold patent medicines.

Gröll's main importance for this study lies in the fact that he was to be the publisher of Ignacy Krasicki (1735–1801), although almost nothing is known of the relations between Krasicki and his publisher. Gröll is rarely mentioned in Krasicki's voluminous correspondence, except when Krasicki complained to third parties of misprints in his published works. However, this state of affairs is hardly to be wondered at, since Krasicki was never a "professional" writer trying to make a living by his pen. The "starveling author" was only beginning to make an appearance in Poland, and relations such as those prevailing in London between Alexander Pope and his publisher Curll were out of the question in eighteenth-century Warsaw.

Important though Gröll's contribution was to the revival of Polish literature under King Stanislas, the true reason for the revival was the appearance of a number of gifted and enlightened writers. Among them, pride of place must be given to Ignacy Krasicki, called the "Prince of Poets" by his contemporaries. He was the most representative and most "Augustan" poet of his time.

II   *The* Polish Monitor

Krasicki came from a well-connected family of Polish landed gentry. The family owned a country estate, but was not wealthy, and Krasicki realized early in life that only two professions were open to him: the Church, or the Army (the Law or Medicine were still not respectable). He chose to enter the Church, and his choice was to be well rewarded—at least in terms of worldly success. After studying at the Jesuit College in Lwów from 1743 to 1750, Krasicki was ordained into the priesthood in 1751. He then spent over a year in Rome, and began his career as a writer when King Stanislas invited him in 1764 to become editor of one of the first literary periodicals to be published in Warsaw.

This was the *Polish Monitor* (established 1763), one of the instruments by which King Stanislas hoped to initiate a number of social and other reforms, and cultivate public taste. The king himself wrote essays for the *Monitor,* but the journal was for the most part closely modelled on the *Tatler* and the *Spectator,* the series of essays written by Addison and Steele, published in London between 1709 and 1711. Their essays were of an improving and moralizing kind, written in a way calculated to amuse and please the reader. The essays functioned by deriding excesses or follies of which the essayists disapproved. Both periodicals contributed to the powerful flood of moralizing that swept across eighteenth-century Europe, for they became widely popular in translation: a French version appeared in 1714, and translations into German and Russian soon followed.[4] The wide circulation of the *Tatler* and *Spectator* essays meant that Addison and Steele were partly responsible for teaching "respect for law, common sense, and other bourgeois virtues" to the middle classes of all Europe.[5]

Significantly, the *Polish Monitor*—though deriving in large part from the English originals—did not appear in Warsaw until some fifty years later. This delay is yet another symptom of the isolation of "Saxon" Poland from Western culture until the election of King Stanislas.

Krasicki accepted the king's invitation, and edited the *Monitor* until 1768, when his absence from Warsaw made it imperative that the editing be entrusted to someone else. However, Krasicki continued to contribute essays and translations, and in 1772, for example, the entire contents of the *Monitor* were his. His method in producing the *Monitor* essays was one frequently used by eighteenth-century writers—that of "adaptation" of other people's work. Just as the eighteenth-century theater in Poland and Russia was crowded with adaptations and imitations of Molière,[6] so in his essays, Krasicki was following a well-established principle, and (as he pointed out) they were "adapted as far as possible to the circumstances and customs of our country."

The essays adumbrate almost all the opinions, topics and themes that Krasicki was later to develop at greater length in his satires, epistles, novels, plays and poetry. So we find him in the pages of the *Monitor* deriding the follies and vices of contemporary society, mocking superstition and reaction, or holding forth on matters of graver import such as legislation, the administration of justice, politics and education. Like Voltaire, Krasicki never hesitated to say the same thing twice, or a dozen times, if he believed it needed to be said.

III   *The Writer's Medium*

Several of the *Monitor* essays contain early statements of Krasicki's views on language—the writer's medium. Along with his more enlightened contemporaries, Krasicki was well aware that the Polish language had fallen into a condition of neglect and decay parallel to that which was to be found in other aspects of Polish life. Under the Saxon kings, Poland had been a Tower of Babel: the kings and their court spoke German, the aristocracy affected French, and education and the administration were conducted in Latin. Only the provincial gentry and the peasants still used Polish.

Voices warning against this neglect had been heard as early as the 1740's, condemning the frequent adoption of foreign words and phrases, fashionable jargon, provincialisms and other elements that marred the Polish language. Konarski's reflections on ways to improve style appeared in 1741, and other writers who published their views on preserving, improving and purifying their national language included many of Krasicki's contemporaries.[7] The same concern for one's own language was being felt at this time all over Europe, from Swift in London to Catherine the Great in St. Petersburg.

Krasicki's first statement on the subject appeared in the tenth issue of the *Monitor* (1765), when he declared that the Polish language "once wealthy, is nowadays despised and held in the utmost contempt. Surely this is the first time a nation should be ashamed of its own language!" He protests that a foreigner visiting Poland would be justified in believing that the French language was Poland's own, or in supposing that Polish consists of a "variety of miscellaneous languages combined together." Here Krasicki is attacking the stylistic mannerism known as the "macaronic" style, in which words and phrases in a foreign language (usually Latin) were interlarded into Polish. The macaronic style had been much favored by writers and orators of the late Baroque, who believed it was both elevated and ornamental.

Next, Krasicki enumerates some of the reasons for the fashionable contempt in which Polish was held: people protest, he says, that it is not as "expressive" as French, and that there are few books written and published in Polish. But he dismisses these charges by pointing out that "it is not the fault of a language if few books be written in it—but the fault of the writers."

Not, of course, that foreign languages should be disregarded. For all his disapproval of French where Polish was more appropriate, Krasicki was thoroughly a man of his time in his admiration for the finest products of French literature and culture. His critical writings and personal letters abound with admiring references to a wide range of French authors, from Rabelais and Molière to Voltaire and Mme. de Sevignée, and he evidently believed that the only literatures superior to French were those of classical antiquity. In the same essay, Krasicki urges that Poland needs translations from foreign literatures, since they would contribute to forming a Polish language that would be both correct and flexible—an ideal for which Krasicki always strived.

As befits the pages of the *Monitor*—the aim of which was always to divert as well as instruct—Krasicki suggests a solution to the problem: women should be encouraged to "scold and nag" their husbands in foreign languages, and reserve Polish for terms of endearments.

A year later, Krasicki returns to the same topic though with a different approach: now he is more concerned with propagating Polish, and suggests there should be a return to the "Slavonic" language from which he held Polish to be derived. He believes that recourse to this ancient tongue would enrich the contemporary language. He therefore urges writers to go back for models to the Polish authors of the sixteenth century "Golden Age." The best writers of the earlier period had, after all, succeeded in forging a vernacular of remarkable strength and clarity.

Krasicki had an additional reason for urging a return to the sixteenth century for models in literature and language. As he well knew, the poetry of the Polish Renaissance—best exemplified in the poetry of Jan Kochanowski (who died in 1584)—was a powerful link between the Augustan age of the eighteenth century, and the Augustan age of Classical Rome. The most characteristic writers of all three ages set a high value on the same things in writing and in life: decorum, elegance, common sense, good taste, wit. All tried in their writings to improve standards and critical values. They had all written in the same, or similar genres—sat-

ires, pastoral poetry, epigrams, epistles. Significantly, Warsaw
printers started issuing new editions of the poetry of Kochanowski
in the 1770's. Krasicki's cult of the earlier poet is only briefly
touched upon in the *Monitor* essays, but is more directly and
clearly expressed in later works. There will be occasion to refer to
Kochanowski in this study.

By urging the study and imitation of earlier Polish writers, Krasicki is expressing his belief that in this way contemporary authors
would help propagate their own language and free it from stylistic flaws inherited (as pointed out above) from the late Baroque
and the despised Saxon age. Krasicki denounced the literature of
the previous period in terms not unlike those of Dr. Johnson condemning the poetry of Cowley, and singles out for particular
blame the "conceits, heraldic allusions, involved allegories, exaggerated metaphors and graphomania."

Not all Krasicki's contributions to the *Monitor* were critical or
condemnatory. He also took it upon himself to provide readers
with advice on how to write well (i.e. in an Augustan manner).
He of course knew Horace's "Ars poetica," and Boileau's *l'Art
poétique* (1674), as well as other manuals of instruction on the
"art of poetry." Such manuals were also published in Poland, and
Krasicki probably knew, for example, that by Waclaw Rzewuski,
published in 1762. Like all the writers of these poetic manuals,
Krasicki places a high value on writing that is "clear, easily
grasped, well-ordered, natural rather than artificial." In making
this statement Krasicki indicates that he shares the view of other
eighteenth-century writers, to whom the "natural" in art was not
the Romantic conception of the term, but rather the antithesis of
the "unnatural" or abnormal.

He who aspires to write well must, first of all, know of what he
writes. Horace had similarly urged would-be poets to examine
their mental resources before starting to write, and urged them to
"choose a subject within their powers." Nor was this all: a writer
must possess the ability to express himself while bearing in mind
all the time that "clarity of style and charming simplicity are cardinal virtues in any kind of writing."

Contemporary writers throughout Europe would have agreed
with Krasicki on all the points he made in the *Monitor* essays
about writing, and the writing of poetry particularly. In these essays, published at the start of his career as a writer, Krasicki sets

forth with characteristic clarity, good-humor, common sense and irony all the principles that rule in his later writings. Everywhere, in all the various genres Krasicki practised over the three decades that made up his life as a poet and novelist, we shall see him striving (and succeeding brilliantly for the most part) to entertain and instruct his fellow men just as he strove in the *Monitor* essays —though on a much larger scale.

CHAPTER 2

The Debut

K RASICKI'S first original long poem was *Myszeidos* (*The Battle of Mice in Ten Cantos*) published by Gröll in Warsaw in 1775. The poem is a characteristic example of the mock-heroic, in which Krasicki demonstrates his familiarity with and admiration for classical epic poetry, its rules and conventions—by deliberately reducing those rules and conventions to the ridiculous. Like innumerable other poets of the Age of Enlightenment, Krasicki is offering "elegantly affectionate homage" to a literary genre he regarded as irrelevant to his own age.[1]

The mock-heroic was a most suitable genre for a poet's debut. Krasicki was very properly following in the Augustan tradition which held that a poet should begin his career in a "low" genre before proceeding to a higher kind. Virgil was believed to have established the tradition by starting with the mock-heroic poem *The Gnat*, a parade of elevated diction describing the undeserved death of a gnat at the hands of a shepherd, its obsequies, and subsequent reappearance as a ghost. Alexander Pope first ventured into print with his *Pastorals* (1709), another comparatively "low" kind of poetry.

The belief that there is a hierarchy of literary forms, some elevated and prestigious, others low and even disreputable, was demolished by the Romantic writers of the early nineteenth century. No self-respecting poet today thinks it necessary to make his debut in a "low" genre before venturing on an elegy, ode or epic poem. We hold that other things are of unquestionably greater importance in poetry: form and content matter today, unconstricted by the application of abstract rules handed down from antiquity. Present-day readers are interested primarily in a writer's performance, not in the form of work in which he has produced.

In the eighteenth century, however, writers, their readers and the critics were convinced that distinctions needed to be made between various kinds of literature. Writing (and reading) began by considering the work in hand in the light of certain recognized structures: it was an elegy, an ode, a satire or something else, and each form had qualities generally agreed upon in advance by an authority, who might have been anyone from Aristotle to Boileau. The entire concept provided a rational and practical guide to the art of writing, and the genres were supported by an immense amount of critical theory. This did not necessarily mean the slavish imitation of a collection of inert models, formulae or patterns. Eighteenth-century writers in all the genres were highly conscious of literary tradition, of the value of suitable and appropriate subjects, and the "rules" assisted them to know precisely how a subject could best be treated. Poems were artifacts, produced by men with particular intentions in mind when they sat down to compose.[2] Poetry was not yet an inspired, often mysterious and fragmentary upsurge from a poet's psyche.

An additional advantage of the system of literary genres was that familiarity with the system provided poets and their readers with common ground. The poets' knowledge of genres, acquired through a classical education and assiduous study of the ancient authors meant that poets need waste no time experimenting: a style and poetic diction appropriate to the subject were laid down in advance—elevated style, lofty diction and elaborate figures of speech were required by epic or tragedy. In satire or mock-heroic, a lower style and diction were proper. It was not necessary for poets to find their own individual "voice," although of course the major poets did.

In a similar way, the reading public of the age—equipped as it was with an education and literary taste similar to those of the writers—was immediately able to identify the level on which a poet was writing, and how he expected the poem to be read. Readers possessed standards of critical judgment which they could apply to any work of art, and judge it accordingly. The existence of these standards and the tradition they stood for was one of the primary reasons for the Romantic revolt—and the reason why Romantic poets like Wordsworth (and Mickiewicz in Poland)[3] were faced with the task of creating *ab ovo* a taste for their own poetry.

Krasicki's choice of the mock-heroic throws light on the reading habits that prevailed in Poland in the 1770's. Proper appreciation of this genre presupposes a good deal of familiarity with the genuine heroic epic poetry that is being satirized. Indeed, the mockery can only be relished to the full by readers well versed in the original genre in whose august shade the mock-heroic stands. Krasicki evidently expected his readers to possess this familiarity, and the fact that they did is attested by the three further editions of *The Battle of Mice* called for during his lifetime (1778, 1780, 1796).

In setting out to write a poem in which the protagonists include mice, Krasicki had a classical model in *The Battle of Frogs and Mice*, a poem long attributed to Homer, in which small creatures are substituted for the human warriors of epic, and the action is described in a high style that is deliberately inappropriate for the "lowness" of the narrative.

I *Augustan Fantasy*

The background of Krasicki's poem is the legendary kingdom of King Popiel, situated on Lake Gopło—about a hundred miles northwest of present-day Warsaw. According to ancient chronicles, this lake had been the site of the first Polish state during the prehistoric period. But by Krasicki's time the veracity of the chronicles was challenged by historians. To rational and enlightened minds, the uncertainties of ancient history, including that of the Bible itself, rendered it a subject that merited little serious attention.

When the poem starts, King Popiel is persuaded by his favorite cat, Mewgrowler, to expel all the mice from the kingdom. When Gristlebite, king of the mice, hears this news, he calls for a general mobilization of his subjects against their enemies, the cats. A battle follows, and the mice are defeated, although Popiel's daughter loses Lapcustard, her favorite cat, in the action. The obsequies of Lapcustard are described with loving particularity in Canto IV.

Gristlebite flees the scene of the mice's defeat, and takes refuge in the hut of a sinister witch. She assists him to return to his defeated army of mice, but during the journey home, Gristlebite falls into the hands of the cats. They prepare to burn him at the stake, though the witch saves the situation by throwing snuff at the cats. In the outbreak of sneezing that follows, Gristlebite makes good his escape.

After successfully undertaking an arduous journey home, Gristlebite calls for a second battle against the cats. This leads to a heroic duel between himself and Mewgrowler, in which the latter is slain and the mice triumph. They march upon King Popiel who has been deserted by his fawning courtiers, and devour him.

Whether or not this plot contains hidden satire directed by Krasicki against the monarchy, or against the conflict between the Polish Senate and gentry (as has been suggested by scholars and others since 1801)[4] is, of course, irrelevant to the poetry. The true meaning of *The Battle of Mice* lies elsewhere. In the first place, Krasicki's plot, or "fable," provided him with ample opportunity for mocking all the regular paraphernalia of classical epic as employed by Homer and Virgil. He begins with the mythical background proper to epic poetry: then come the heroic battle and duel between two famed warriors, followed by supernatural intervention in the hero's adventures (the witch) and a Homeric stratagem (the witch confounding Gristlebite's enemies with snuff, reminiscent of the snuff with which Belinda confounds her enemy in Alexander Pope's *The Rape of the Lock* [1714, translated into Polish in 1788]); the long and arduous journey undertaken by the poem's hero, during which he overcomes apparently insuperable difficulties. Funeral rites and lamentations are provided by Lapcustard's obsequies. Krasicki's sly use of all these elevated subjects in a low context (applied to cats and mice) was a part of his poetic technique.

If this were all, however, the poem would be little more than a skilful parody. But Krasicki does more than mock the external trappings of an obsolete genre. In addition to the "machinery," he also introduces many of the stylistic devices proper to epic. He offers extended "heroic" similes (Gristlebite is compared in an eight-line simile to Bajazet in captivity to Tamburlaine), vices and virtues are personified (with the aid of capital letters), apostrophes and invocations are made to Fate, Fortune or the gods of Classical mythology; characters deliver long harangues and speeches, and examples of elevated diction appear in the form of catalogs of resounding names, adding pomp and magnificence to genuine epic. In addition, the author's own voice is heard from time to time, urging us to pity or admire this or that character. He will hold up the narrative to deliver moral *sententiae*, intended (in an epic) to demonstrate the poet's omniscience and wisdom.

Even the structure of *The Battle of Mice* is classically heroic, being divided into ten major episodes (catonic). Although Krasicki employs octavo (eight-line) stanzas instead of the more usual hexameter, his license to do so was afforded by the much-admired seventeenth-century translation into Polish of Tasso's *Jerusalem Liberated* by Piotr Kochanowski (Cracow, 1618). Although not particularly Augustan, this poem is eminently heroic.

The mockery inherent in *The Battle of Mice* depends, as does the mockery in Pope's *The Rape of the Lock*, on the "diminuition of size and time, in the meanness of the facts, and incongruity of the epic manner for its narration." [5] Krasicki was as skilled as Pope in exploiting the various stylistic devices characteristic of both classical and Augustan poetry. Not, however, that these devices—which occur variously in items of poetic diction, of prosody and of structure—were merely echoes or imitations. Basically, they served to provide Krasicki with a well-ordered and firm structure, inside which he set the fantastic, legendary world of a prehistorical Poland inhabited by kings and witches, by cats and mice that talk and act like human beings. The diction, prosody and structure transform this fantastic material by controlling it, and the poem becomes an example of art controlling fantasy, or form controlling content—a process that is characteristically Augustan.

Despite the fantastic characters and events in King Popiel's kingdom on the lake, the settings are not fantastic. They are Augustan, and Krasicki makes sure that they are so by using various kinds of poetic diction. For example, King Popiel's castle is situated on a Lake Gopło which the Romantic poet and dramatist Juliusz Slowacki would not have recognized. To Slowacki, who set his fantastic tragedy *Balladyna* (1839) on the shores of this same lake, Gopło was a region bordering on the magical forest of Shakespeare's *Midsummer Night's Dream*, with a hint of the prehistoric kingdom of *King Lear*, populated respectively by elves, fairies, water-sprites, clowns, lovers and murderers.

But in Krasicki's poem, the lake is situated in an elegant, well-kept landscape of "expansive and fertile fields," with "ancient birch-trees" in whose branches "various birds" find refuge. The hills and valleys around are "green and fertile," and form an "agreeable prospect," in which the fields are "adorned with various flowers" and thickets "planted as though on purpose." Man's hand is everywhere apparent, as it was in many eighteenth-century gardens, from which the wild, the unkempt and the untamed were banished.

A "diverting echo" can be heard, as a "sanguine shepherd" plays his rustic flute under a "thick bush." Popiel's castle stands on an "ornate island," "roses crown its copper gates," and "crowds of nymphs are guardians of the fortress." Here, and throughout the rest of the poem, Krasicki is showing a typically Augustan concern with imposing his own civilized intellect on the scene, and he does so primarily by means of the diction he uses. This is the function of these neutral, even colorless epithets, which are not intended to modify their nouns in a striking, dramatic or revealing manner, but to single out, rather, some obvious attribute implicit in the noun, or to name some permanent characteristic. Their deliberately conventional flavor is a signal that reassures the reader that no special reaction is required. The fantasy is under control.

The inert quality of the epithets in *The Battle of Mice* is typical of much eighteenth-century poetry, especially descriptive or "Nature" poetry, and explains why this poetry is something of an acquired taste. Readers nowadays feel that this diction provides no fresh observation. The poet is not really looking at the landscape, hence the absence of the strongly visual quality to which we are accustomed in the descriptive poetry of the Romantics.

But in mock-heroic poetry, dead epithets serve a special purpose—that of the "continuous repression of the emotional by the intellectual." [6] This repression contributes also to the undercurrent of serenity which is a feature of Augustan poetry. Other examples used by Krasicki in this poem are "a squeaking nation" and "a squeaking kind" (the mice), phrases that correspond exactly to Pope's use of "the fishy kind," and similar expressions.

Not that Krasicki's predilection for neutral epithets was exclusively negative and repressive. The epithets are used also to provide a background for coloring of a different sort—that which comes from the brilliance of verbal wit. Moreover, the inert epithets are accompanied by other kinds of diction, grouped around appropriate characters, incidents or passages of description. They include loan-words from other languages, diminutives and also elevated words, such as compounds. The cats and King Popiel's courtiers are consistently associated with foreign words. Krasicki's protests in the *Monitor* essays against the excessive use of French in Warsaw drawing-rooms and elsewhere, foreshadow his satirical use of French at Popiel's court, as he applies such genteel words as "amant," "faworyt," and "respekt" to cats.

Diminutives, for which few English equivalents exist, gave Krasicki another kind of diction. These are the "tender" words, much affected by his contemporaries in pastoral poetry, and which led to a decline in this genre. Such words were particularly despised by the Romantics, who exiled them altogether from serious poetry. The obsequies of the pet cat Lapcustard are described by a large number of words such as "little tiny coffin," "teeny-weeny hands," "diminutive animals" and "tomb-lets."

Yet another kind of poetic diction appears in Krasicki's use of elevated words in a low context. To append such titles as "Absolute Prince," "Chancellor," or "Marshal" to cats and mice immediately reduce the titles to absurdity. In the same way, Krasicki's catalogs of resounding geographical names (Caspian, Libyan, Arabian, Caucasian, Moorish) are diminished to the mock-heroic level by their application to—rats. So, too, the elevated compound words ("hundred-headed," "swift-flying" and the like) used by Homer to lend grandeur to the epic poem, become equally ludicrous.

II   Patterns in Poetry

Syntax has justly been called "the groundwork of the poet's art." [7] This was certainly the case in Krasicki's art, and he took an evident delight in the subtle effects to be gained from syntactical and grammatical patterns, expecting that his readers would do so too. A conspicuous syntactical item in *The Battle of Mice* is the "golden line," which Dryden once defined as a line consisting of "two substantives and two adjectives, with a verb betwixt to keep the peace." This arrangement was much favored in classical Latin poetry. Catullus introduced twenty-one "golden lines" into a passage of 400 lines, Horace appropriated the "golden line" from epic poetry and transferred it to his lyrics, while Virgil considered the device especially suited for expressing a "powerful sentiment or majestic tableau." [8] The "golden line" became a constant stylistic feature in the poetry of Ovid, Lucan, Claudian and others.

Eighteenth-century Augustan poets were quick to adopt the "golden line" into their own poetry, and examples can be found on every page of the petrified epics that litter the period, from Voltaire's *Henriade* (1724) to Lomonosov's *Peter the Great* (1760–1761). From the epic the "golden line" soon spread to other kinds of poetry. Here are some examples: in Horace's version of the country mouse visiting the town mouse (*Satires* II, 6, 102–104) two golden lines in succession emphasize the splendor of the town mouse's feast:

> rubro ubi cocco
> tincta super lectos canderet vestis eburnos,
> multaque de magna superessent fercula cena

> (where draperies dyed crimson blazed on
> ivory couches, and many courses remained
> from a great banquet)

> plaudentem nigra figit sub nube columbam
> (Virgil, *Aenid* V, 516)

> (he pierced the weeping dove under a black sky)

> The lonely woodcock haunts the wat'ry glade
> (Pope)

> The clam'rous lapwings feel the leaden death
> (Pope)

> Et d'un nectar vermeil rougit les froides ondes
> (Delille)

> C'est le boeuf matinal qui suit le soc tranchant
> (Delille)

Examples are also to be found in Russian epic poetry of the eighteenth century, such as Lomonosov's *Peter the Great*, mentioned above.

Admittedly, such deliberate arrangements of works strike us today as artificial (to say the least), and modern grammarians have described it (in Latin) as a "distorted and unnatural order of words." [9] But to the ears of eighteenth-century readers, attuned to classical poetry, it must have held unmistakable resonances.

Moreover, the highly flexible word-order of which the Polish language is capable, and the absence of intrusive definite and indefinite articles, made that language still more easily adaptable to the golden line in its classical form than either English or French. The device came to be regarded as a "favorite pseudo-classical means of monumental expression." [10]

Krasicki's use of the majestic "golden line" in *The Battle of Mice* is on a par with his use of other characteristic features of Augustan poetic diction and stylistic devices that derive from the epic. It was yet another means of emphasizing the absurdity of his mock-heroic narrative by adorning it with as many elements as possible of the epic. He employs the "golden line" in several ways in the poem, always with a strong medial caesura that divides the line into balancing parts. There are lines balanced around a verb (as in Dryden's definition):

And crowds of nymphs were guardians of the fortress (I, 72),

A monarch's sins are his country's poison (I, 80),

or around a particle:

A worthy capital of such great monarchs (I, 37),

or around the caesura alone:

The horrible uproar (of) miaowing cats (III, 81).

Elsewhere Krasicki builds his golden lines by framing them between epithet and noun (II, 98, 120) as in Virgil's

magnum reginae sed enim miseratus amorem (*Aeneid* VI, 28),
yet, sympathizing with the queen in her great love.

He also follows the model provided by Latin poetics to the extent of carefully avoiding epithets at the end of lines. This avoidance is too consistent to be required merely by the demands of rhyme, and in any case Krasicki's virtuosity in the handling of rhyme (impossible to demonstrate here) was certainly equal to Pope's.

He displays a corresponding fondness for other figures of classical poetics, such as zeugma, in which a word is linked to two others, appropriately to the first, less so to the second. The figure has been called characteristic of the poetry of Virgil.[11] An example from the *Aeneid* is "fugam Dido sociosque parabat" (Dido made ready for flight, made ready her companions too). Pope's line "A wit with dunces, and a dunce with wits" is echoed by Krasicki's "We rule the world and women us," "the cat claws the rat, the rat bites the cat," and others.

The use of zeugma, and other devices such as asyndeton (in

which words or phrases are linked together without connectives)
and anaphora (in which a series of lines all begin with the same
word) served a dual purpose in Krasicki's poem. First, they provided his readers with agreeable echoes of familiar originals, on
the Aristotelian principle that imitation revives the pleasure of the
original in a reader's mind.[12] But they are also devices of economy,
which enabled Krasicki to pack more meaning and intensity into a
single line than his less skilled contemporaries could. This was one
of Pope's special achievements, too, which set him above his imitators. For one of the main features of classical and Augustan poetry is its economy of means. The poets of both ages knew that
"brevity is the soul of wit."

Even the overall structure of *The Battle of Mice* is classical, in
the way that Krasicki demonstrates throughout the same concern
for balance and proportion between the component parts as did
the Latin poets of antiquity. In their longer poems, there is almost
invariably an inner balance between parts. The proportion of oral
(spoken) or of descriptive passages is always larger than the
amount of narrative, which is kept to a minimum. As Pope declared in the preface to his translation of the *Iliad:* "It is hardly
credible, in a work of such length, how small a number of lines
are employ'd in the narration." Krasicki was equally well aware of
this peculiarity of classical epics, and it is not surprising that the
narrative parts of *The Battle of Mice* are reduced, more often
than not, to single lines placed between the long passages of description, battle scenes and speeches. Several purely decorative
and essentially static episodes, such as the funeral rites of Lapcustard, extend to eighty lines and more.

Proportion operates within the poem too; sections of equal importance are dealt with in precisely the same number of lines. The
two battles between the mice and the cats in cantos III and IX,
respectively, both occupy 112 lines. The introductory part, leading
to King Popiel elevating the cat Mewgrowler to favorite at Court,
corresponds exactly to the part following Mewgrowler's death in
battle (again, 112 lines each).

Nowhere does Krasicki draw attention to these examples of
classical equilibrium and inner symmetry. Indeed, they have gone
unnoticed by scholarship to the present day, though critics have
observed the symmetrical structure of other of Krasicki's works,
such as *The Battle of Monks* and its sequel, which contain pre-

cisely the same number of lines. Even though the symmetry is inconspicuous in *The Battle of Mice*, Krasicki presumably felt it was necessary to the poem's total effect. Besides, he was following in the footsteps of Horace, whose *Odes* (Book III) contains thirty poems, divided into three groups, each group containing 336 lines.

Yet another feature of classical poetry which Augustan writers admired and imitated was the art of transition between the parts of a long poem. Most Roman poets cultivated this art, though Ovid—with his carmen perpetuum—was considered the most skilled practitioner of transitions. Krasicki's contemporary, the poet editor, and critic Franciszek Dmochowski, drew attention to the importance of effecting skilful transitions in the *Art of Versifying* (1788), referring to Boileau as his authority. One of the most striking features to eighteenth-century readers of Macpherson's imitation epic *Ossian* was the lack of transition between its parts: this was considered a truly original feature, and one that guaranteed its claim to be genuinely "primitive."

Krasicki's transitions are effected with Augustan ingenuity and skill. Sometimes he uses such acceptable conjunctions as "meanwhile" to provide a link. More reminiscent of Ovid are the thematic transitions, as in canto IV: after describing the grief of Popiel's daughter at the death of her cat Lapcustard, Krasicki leads into a catalog enumerating the charms of the late cat while he was still alive, then refers back to the princess's grief and that of the hypocritical mourners. They decide to afford Lapcustard a splendid funeral, which immediately begins in the next stanza.

Transitions occur between the individual cantos also: time is ingeniously used to effect the transition between cantos III and IV. The former concludes with the coming of night, the latter opens with praise of golden-haired Phoebus heralding dawn. Similarly, canto VIII ends with Gristlebite setting forth on his heroic journey, and canto IX opens with the poet reflecting on the benefits and disadvantages of foreign travel in general. Krasicki then turns his attention back to Gristlebite, whose journey is now well under way. In fact, the whole poem is welded together by means of these almost imperceptible but very classical transitions. The final "classical" feature of Krasicki's poetry, evident in *The Battle of Mice*—and in all his later poetry too—is his avoidance of run-on lines, generally shunned by Augustan writers, though much cultivated by Baroque poets of the previous era.

Krasicki's predilection for figures of prosody, his concern with syntax, symmetry and proportion, suggest that he possessed to a high degree the "order and precision of a grammarian," and "the style of a craftsman," all of which combined to make the truly Roman poets of antiquity.[13] None of these elements was introduced merely for the sake of effect, for decoration, or to promote admiration for the poet's verbal and syntactical ingenuity. They are essential parts of Krasicki's means of expression—not a superficial skill used to arrange a verbal surface. They lie half hidden under the wit and satire that are the most immediately striking feature of *The Battle of Mice*, and they contribute to making Krasicki the pre-eminent literary stylist of Augustan Poland.

CHAPTER 3

The Battle of Monks, *and its Sequel*

K RASICKI rose to high rank in the Catholic Church: he was
ordained a Bishop in 1766, and became Archbishop of
Gniezno in 1795—yet his writings make little or no mention of
religion. His poetry very rarely gives utterance to any kind of religious sensibility, while manifestations of mystical fervor (as had
been made by many of the Baroque poets) are as foreign to Krasicki's nature as they were to Voltaire's. No doubt Krasicki was
sincerely pious, even devout: but the supernatural aspects of religion such as miracles, mysteries or the prophetic were alien to his
enlightened, rational views. Krasicki was here in agreement with
the progressive views of his age, which regarded monastic obscurantism (for example) as an abhorrent survival of the preceding
period of darkness.

This was the topic Krasicki took for his next mock-heroic poem
Monachomachia, (The Battle of Monks, 1778), in which he ridi-
cules the monastic orders in Poland. At first sight, the idea of a
Bishop of the Catholic Church satirizing monks for stupidity, glut-
tony, idleness and drunkenness is outrageous. However, anti-
clerical satire flourished greatly in Western Europe during the
Age of Enlightenment, and the number of anti-religious lampoons
and satires published during the period has without exaggeration
been called "incredible." [1] The targets were twofold: on the one
hand, superstition, on the other, the despotic, brutalizing nature
of the ecclesiastical organizations themselves. Krasicki knew such
examples of anti-clerical satire as Boileau's *Le Lutrin* (1683) and
Gresset's *Ver-Vert* (1734)—a poem in which nuns quarrel over
the ownership of a parrot. Gresset was a Jesuit priest when he
published his mock-heroic poem, and the circumstances surrounding its publication are still somewhat mysterious. Gresset claimed
afterwards that he had nothing to do with its publication, then
declared that in any case it was published without his approval.

However, the Catholic Church authorities raised no serious objections to *Ver-Vert* because Gresset did not attack theological doctrines or fundamental dogma.

I   The Battle of Monks

Krasicki published *The Battle of Monks* under equally mysterious circumstances, and anonymously: but the poem's authorship did not remain a secret for long. It deals at length (six cantos, 108 stanzas) with a struggle between Dominican and Carmelite monks, urged on by the Spirit of Envy, and concluding with a general reconciliation and a drinking bout. Unlike *The Battle of Mice,* which treats "low" characters with all the stylistic pomp of an epic, *The Battle of Monks* brings venerable characters down to ridicule and contempt.

After a traditional epic flourish, in which Krasicki announces his intention ("Civil war I sing,/A war ferocious, without weapons or swords,/Of barefoot knights"), he proceeds to carry it out with all the ingenuity and wit at his command. The action of the poem takes place in a provincial town somewhere in Poland, which Krasicki discreetly declines to name, consisting of "three taverns, four ruined gates, nine monasteries, and—here and there—little houses." Krasicki does not date the action either: but it would seem to occur before 1773, since the Jesuit order in Poland was dissolved in that year (the order was revived throughout Europe early in the nineteenth century).

In this derelict, though typical setting, "reverend stupidity has been settled for ages," and the disproportionate number of monasteries is in accord with the facts; by the end of the seventeenth century there were over 600 monasteries and convents in Poland. The "delightful abode of holy idlers" is soon disturbed by the Serpent of Strife, also known as Eris, a female in black, with serpents in her hair and a fiery torch in her hand. When Eris catches sight of the "sweet paradise of monks," she cries out with rage, scatters sparks from her torch over the monastery roofs and towers, and the monks, though "somnolent with lethargy," awaken in alarm.

First to awaken is the Prior, Father Hilary, and Krasicki remarks in an aside that this was the first time the Prior had been awake early enough to see the dawn. The monks crowd into the monastery refectory, and their first concern is whether "robbers

have got into the cellars?/Whether our barrels, flasks and bottles
have run dry?" Reassured by "crystal clear vodka," and a portion
of Torun pie, the monastery's venerable Doctor "blinked, puffed
and sneezed." The superstitious monks take this for a good omen,
and proceed one by one to offer advice on the proper course to
follow in the coming dispute with the Carmelites.

Individual monks now give voice: Father Honorat supports his
advice with learned quotations, Father Gaudenty urges "Let us
strike while we are strong!" but the pacific Father Pancracy suggests settling the dispute by a debate. But even as they are setting
forth their arguments, the rest of the monks sink back into the
arms of Morpheus, who "sows sweet sleep and desirable dreams"
among them all.

Canto II opens with a distressing omen in the neighboring Carmelite monastery, as Father Raymond trips on a doorstep. Well
aware of the prophetic meaning of this accident, all the Carmelite
monks gather in their refectory, and incidentally provide Krasicki
with the opportunity of enumerating resounding names: Elias of
St. Barbara, Mark of the Trinity, Jan of St. Peter of Alcantare,
Hermenegildus of the Seven Sorrows, Raphael of St. Peter, and so
on. Then Father Gaudenty of the Dominicans enters, bringing
with him an embassy to challenge the Carmelites to a debate.

The Carmelites accept this challenge, and when the embassy
has departed, another council ensues: Father Makary advises
against war, Father Cherubim quotes examples, Father Seraphim
wishes to tempt Fate, Father Panufcy sends out spies: Krasicki
sums up the situation by commenting: "The old are afraid of war,
but the young long for it." The dinner bell brings the council to an
abrupt conclusion and "Out they all rushed, as though being pur-
sued."

Canto III opens with a parade of auctorial wisdom in which
Krasicki contrasts wise men of old who praised bread and water,
with the present day when temperance is no longer fashionable,
and "wise men drink as much as everybody else." He adds: "Mead
that's good gives thoughts vitality,/Wine cheers wretched hearts."
From these statements there is a classical transition to the reverend fathers who themselves give proof of the statements. On
emerging from the refectory after dinner, Father Gervazy suggests challenging their foes to a drinking contest. Father Hilary
warns against this, however: "I know them well," he cries, "and so

does Father Anthony:/We hold our drink well, but they hold it still better."

Another manner of settling the dispute (inflamed by the Serpent of Strife) is proposed by Father Elizeusz, who declares that the heart of the matter lies in study: "The times of happy simplicity are gone,/A man must study, the Golden Age is passed." Krasicki then pays a compliment to King Stanislas by having Father Elizeusz address the king: "O thou, seated on the throne of Poland!/Despiser of mead, and uninterested in wine . . . Your taste is for books, while your cellars are in ruins."

Elizeusz reveals to the startled monks that the monastery contains a library, "said to be located somewhere in the attics," and suggests they may find suitable weapons there. Since no one knows where this library is, and no one wishes to take the trouble of seeking it, they decide to leave the search to the lowest hierarchy of lay-brothers, the apothecary and the tailor.

In due course, the lay-brothers come upon a storeroom "mouldering with the years" in the ruins of an ancient tower, and although the ruins threaten to tumble down at any moment, the seekers clamber up the tottering stairs, break a rusty lock and are rewarded by the "delightful sight" of the long-forgotten library.

Meanwhile, the monks continue to fortify themselves with strong liquors which "sweeten cares and appease sorrow," and in which there is both "comfort and profit." The canto ends as the "brothers of peace prepare for war," and canto IV opens with a satirical attack by Krasicki on "Thou, whom no man understood,/ Wandering in your writings as though in a forest," whom "the world once admired, and still celebrates and praises." Not until line 6 does Krasicki name the personage he is attacking as Aristotle, the "ornament of out-dated schools." Krasicki admits it is not the fault of Aristotle that his philosophy has given birth to fools, for the latter are merely "the offspring of an illegitimate bed." A parody of classical epic follows, as Krasicki lists the official names of ranks in the monastic hierarchy to obtain a grotesque effect.

The attack on Aristotle and his rhetoric is explained as the Vice-Regent embarks upon a rhetorical and "philosophical" speech which enables Krasicki to hold up to ridicule the worst excesses of Baroque and Saxon oratory. The Vice-Regent brings together worn-out allegory ("the ship of wisdom"), classical philosophy ("the pearl of the Peripatetic"), astronomy (references to the planets, sun and moon), resounding names ("the Dukes of Ostrog, Counts of Pinczow, the Górka, Tarnowski and Krasicki families, the Bourbon dynasty")—all used to elevate his own learning and virtues. The speech ends, appropriately, with the classical "dixi" (I have spoken) of epic.

The debate is continued in similar terms by Father Lucas, who takes the opposite side, but fails to quote any authorities so that his words are judged "feeble," and they pass in one ear and out the other. Much to everyone's alarm, the third disputant, Father Hyacinth, is interrupted by the sound of drums and trumpets, and at this point Krasicki ends canto IV.

That Krasicki knew very well the enormity of satirizing monks is demonstrated by the opening of the next canto, in which he justifies his proceedings: "Let us respect the wise, the exemplary, the praiseworthy,/And make mock of fools—even though they be reverend." Meanwhile the uproar increases, and Father Hyacinth, after dallying with a "pious lady," enters the refectory to find it a battle-field. Garments and shoes are flying through the air, and Hyacinth is laid flat by a wine-bottle wielded by Father Zeferin. Enraged by this sight, Father Gaudenty tips the Prior off his chair, seizes the Definitor by the cowl, and the latter loses his "last two teeth." Plates and glasses are shattered on "hard heads," and as Gaudenty aims a holy water sprinkler at one of his foes, the water gets into his own eyes, and he is wounded on the head.

As the battle continues to rage, Krasicki stands aside to liken the scene to a streamlet flowing down the "summits of sky-high Alps," which increases in volume as it flows, waxes into a river, and "in violent flow,/It froths, roars and fumes in billows." In a desperate attempt to halt the carnage, the Prior orders a *vitrum gloriosum* (celebrated goblet) be brought, and this object (full of wine), ceremoniously carried in, returns the warring monks to their senses. Krasicki's contemporary readers would have perceived the significance of the goblet at once: when debates in local parliaments (dietines) between the vociferous and argumentative Polish gentry turned into fighting, it was the custom to summon a priest with the Sacrament to restore order.[2]

Krasicki describes the goblet with affectionate care. It is engraved with representations of the four seasons of the year: Spring, with shepherdesses dancing, parishioners at a Summer fair, a priest counting tithes in Autumn, and Winter with its frosts.

The memory of this goblet may well have been responsible for the celebrated center-piece that forms the focal point of the banquet in Mickiewicz's *Pan Tadeusz* (1834) and this hypothesis is rendered all the more likely since Krasicki's complete works (including *The Battle of Monks*) were published in Paris only four years before Mickiewicz's poem was written there.

As the Prior now declares: "The goblet has halted them, and the wine will reconcile." This is the cue for "red-faced, fat Father Czesław" to bring in enormous flasks, and the refectory fills with "vinous perfume." All drink a toast, though Krasicki admits he does not know to whom: but he declares "Had I been among them, I'd have drunk yours, respected Prior," since he, alone among the other characters of the poem, has proved by his example that "Virtue, not robes, makes a monk."

II   *The Sequel*

This outspoken satirical attack, while delighting the public, could not but be offensive to the monastic orders that were its butt—even though *The Battle of Monks* is more comic than satiric. Krasicki's monks, while idle, self-satisfied and over-indulgent in the pleasures of the flesh, are not vicious. In this respect, they differ from the sinister, depraved monks who soon began appearing in popular "Gothic romances," and of whom M. G. Lewis's *Ambrosio, or The Monk* (1796) is best remembered.

Nevertheless, Krasicki thought it proper to publish another poem ostensibly attacking *The Battle of Monks*. This was his *Anti-Battle of Monks* (1780), in which he demonstrates his technical virtuosity by making the new poem exactly the same length as its predecessor. Not, however, that Krasicki recants any of the satirical points he made in the first poem: he was only too well aware that *The Battle of Monks* had made little or no effect on the faults he had attacked. Monastic superstition, obscurantism, pedantry, drunkenness still needed to be attacked.

In the *Anti-Battle*, Krasicki presents the same monastery as before. A copy of *The Battle*, provided by the same Goddess of Envy whose machinations had caused the original war, reaches the hands of the very persons it derided. Their reactions vary: the Doctor merely laughs, for surely the satire cannot apply to him: "Genuine virtue," he remarks complacently, "fears no critics!" Honorat, on the other hand, is outraged: "On reading the first

page, a change came upon him;/Confused, he blushes, turns pale
with rage,/And without finishing the book, he throws it at the
wall," declaring that the author of such profanities must be "a vile
heretic, a Turk, a Jansenist,/An atheist poisoned with the malice
of Hell,/A cheat, who takes advantage of other people's defects."

Honorat hastens to spread news of the book around the monastery. The reverend Fathers, thunderstruck, leave their "pious di-
versions," and attend an argument between Honorat and the
Monastery Librarian, during which the former regrets the "good
old days" when everyone "minded their own business." The Librarian points out that even in the olden days "many a fool found
his way into print." But Honorat is not convinced.

A lyrical meditation on Sleep opens canto III, from which Krasicki makes an elegant transition to the slumbers of Father Gaudenty, unaware of the agitation of the other monks. But the Spirit
of Discord has caught sight of the venerable old monk, she hastens into his cell, "her eyes burning, mouth livid, countenance pal-
lid,/Voice trembling," and succeeds in inspiring Gaudenty with
"rage, despair." Like Hercules ("when he went out to battle with
giants and dragons"), so Gaudenty puts on his monkish hood and
rushes out to do battle.

Night still prevails outdoors, though dawn is at hand; the shout-
ing of monks in dispute can be heard echoing around the monastery, and Honorat joins in, his fury gradually decreasing as "bright
day" appears. An ironical survey of the fate of *The Battle of
Monks* opens canto IV, where Krasicki delivers a warning to
"thieves"—the printers and publishers of his day who pirated editions of his own and other poets' work. Krasicki's publisher in
Warsaw, Gröll, was greatly plagued by his rivals in the field, and
issued a number of "warnings," similar to that of Krasicki.[3]

The monks' copy of *The Battle* now goes from hand to hand:
Father Hyacinth reads it, but fails to recognize his own portrait;
Father Gervazy plots to be revenged on its author, until he hears
—from a pious lady parishioner—that the poet has been seen
"burning in flames at a crossroad." Gervazy then proceeds to the
Dominican monastery, scene of the "battle" of the earlier poem,
and appeals for "cordial unity" in this hour of peril. A general
council follows, adorned with speeches full of Latin and elevated
rhetoric, mythological allusions and false logic. All present agree
that the satirist-poet must be punished—until a four-gallon

pitcher appears, and the monks take turns to imbibe. Gradually the wine sinks, until the pitcher reaches the Doctor. As he drinks the last drops, he starts back in alarm, having caught sight of Truth in person at the bottom. She emerges, and informs the assembled monks that the author of *The Battle* held them up to derision "because he sincerely loves you." "Wit," she continues, "is a weapon often traitorous and harmful,/But sometimes it must be used,/For an apt warning may be hidden in a smile." Truth's last words are particularly apt, since they describe one of the main features of Krasicki's writings—the ever-present desire to "teach while smiling."

For all the wit, irony and poised urbanity of tone in *The Battle of Monks* and its sequel, the two poems are less successful within the mock-heroic genre than *The Battle of Mice*. This is partly because the subject-matter lends itself less readily to poetic treatment. Krasicki had a strong vein of fantasy (by eighteenth-century standards), which sets him above his enlightened contemporaries. To be sure, the fantasy was well controlled (whereas that of de Sade, for instance, was not). Like Pope, whose *The Rape of the Lock* owes much to the fantastic and supernatural Sprites, Krasicki felt at home in a world of the imagination. In his next work, the *Fables*, he returns to just such a world, populated by speaking animals, plants and even objects.

CHAPTER 4

Fabulist

THE idea of bestowing the grace of art upon moralizing seems to recur in periods of high civilization, when society finds general truths about Man, his behavior and human nature to be interesting, and suitable matter for poetry. Aesop's audience for his fables found his way of stating truths about Man in terms of animals and objects was interesting enough in itself: other periods —including our own—find that indirect methods (paradox and the like) are more interesting.

The genre certainly flourished in ancient Athens, and even so eminent an authority as Aristotle found the fable a suitable topic for critical discussion, although he regarded it not as a genre proper, but as an item of rhetoric, a means of persuading by the use of words. Aesop's fables entered Poland in the early sixteenth century, when some two hundred were translated into Polish by Biernat of Lublin in 1522. Aesop soon became a familiar figure in Polish literature, with numerous editions appearing in succession.[1]

The writing of original fables was much practiced in the eighteenth century, when the fables of La Fontaine (1621–1695) gained wide popularity all over Europe, some being translated into Polish by Franciszek Kniaźnin (1750–1807). Not, however, that the writing of fables was easy; as Jonathan Swift remarked, "There is no kind of writing I esteem more than fables, nor anything so difficult to succeed in." John Gay, best remembered for his *The Beggar's Opera*, went as far as to say that "Though fable composition is a kind of writing that appears very easy, I find it the most difficult I ever undertook." Although Krasicki composed two volumes of fables, he had to admit that they did not come "to order."

In the eighteenth century, as the work of Krasicki and his contemporaries constantly remind us, a poet's function was always to teach and to please. Poets were naturally endowed with the authority to teach because their gift of poetry gave them deeper knowledge about Truth, Virtue, Beauty and Decorum than other people possessed. They were therefore under a moral obligation to divulge their knowledge to the rest of society. To be sure, what the poets knew was not always strikingly original, or new: but the concept of originality in literature is, after all, a comparatively recent innovation. Eighteenth-century poets were not affected by the modern craving for "originality" at any price. Their knowledge often amounts to what we might call commonplaces ("The paths of glory lead but to the grave"), clearly and elegantly worded. Yet, as Dr. Johnson justly observed, these are truths of which we need to be reminded from time to time.

Many of Krasicki's contemporaries wrote fables, including Adam Naruszewicz (1735–1796) (some adapted from those of La Fontaine), Stanislaw Trembecki (1739–1812) and J. U. Niemcewicz (1757–1841) (whose fables often conceal political comment). Krasicki's first collection, *Fables and Parables,* appeared in 1779, and although he returns to the fantastic world of *The Battle of Mice,* in which animals spoke, behaved and suffered like human beings, the function of the animals in the fables is no longer merely to assist in a witty parody of serious poetry. Instead, they are used to illustrate Krasicki's own attitudes and ideas concerning a wide range of human weaknesses, foibles, vices and problems of practical morality. Essentially, Krasicki is giving his readers a series of answers to the basic question: "How shall a man live?" Throughout the fables Krasicki adopts an implicitly moral attitude, and by illuminating instances of vanity, folly and weakness is asking us to see ourselves more clearly, even if we might prefer not to.

His "Introduction to the Fables" gives us a warning of what to expect:

> A youth there was, who led a temperate life;
> An aged man, disliking spleen and strife;
> A miser rich, who shared of all he had;
> An author, who of others' fame was glad;
> An honest publican, a cobbler sober,
> A modest soldier, and a gentle robber;
> A public servant thinking not of gain;

A poet too, whose verse gave no one pain—
What tales are these? They may, perhaps, be true,
But I should call them *fables*—wouldn't you? [2]

Although the animals, objects and human types that populate
Krasicki's satires belong in one sense to a fairy-tale world and can
be enjoyed on that level by children, they are also analogues for
human beings, and are therefore endowed with human characteristics. Most fables (not only those of Krasicki) illustrate in dramatic form the everlasting struggle between vice and virtue—and
from time immemorial, as Aesop well knew, vice, tyranny and
cruelty usually triumph. It is the innocent, foolish lamb that is
devoured, or the man who succumbs to flattery that perishes.

From this, it would appear that the satirist's view of human life
is one of pessimism. The moral in many fables is not so much "Be
good," as "Be cunning." This is certainly the case in the world of
Krasicki's fables. But when vice triumphs over the weak, the foolish, or the innocent in a fable, we should read the fable as a warning. Krasicki is reminding us, through his animals and objects,
that Man is a presumptuous, blind and foolish creature, who thoroughly deserves his fate.

The animals that populate fables have another function too.
Traditionally, each species of animal had its own character. Aristotle pointed out, in his *History of Animals,* that

Some are good-tempered, sluggish, and little prone to ferocity, like
the ox; others are quick-tempered, ferocious and unteachable, like the
wild boar; some are intelligent and timid, as the stag and hare; others
are mean and treacherous, as the snake; others are noble and coura-
geous and high-bred, as the lion . . . Some are spirited and affectionate and fawning, as the dog; others are cautious and watchful, as the
goose; some are jealous and self-conceited, as the peacock.

The ancient Greeks believed these were natural qualities, be-
stowed on animals by the gods. The notion survives today, of
course: owls are wise, foxes sly, bees industrious, sheep silly.
Hence, when encountering one of these creatures in a fable, we
expect it to behave in character. The fabulist, remembering that
"brevity is the soul of wit," need not waste time on characterizing
his personages. However, Krasicki's artistry is such that he was
not content with a gallery of stereotypes. He often attributes char-

acteristics other than the conventional ones to his creatures. Cats in his fables, for example, are sometimes marked by their independence, or by hypocrisy, while on other occasions they are self-satisfied, skeptical or philosophical.

The depiction in fables of animals and inanimate objects (vegetables, flowers, plants, trees, coins, articles of dress and so on) has an additional advantage to the fabulist, in that the reader does not become "emotionally involved" with the characters. Relations between animals are naturally on a primitive, direct basis, and to see a mouse perish through ill-considered or foolish behavior is amusing, for it does not remind us of mortality. The problems and dilemmas in which Krasicki places his non-human characters are intended to engage the reader's attention in the moral and intellectual sphere—not the emotional. The pleasure to be gained from a reading of fables is of an intellectual kind.

As already suggested, the essential feature of a fable is brevity and economy of effect. Fables, like epigrams and proverbs (all of which have a moralizing function), are one of the most economical ways of stating an argument and making a point. The brevity is itself part of the intellectual argument, and lends a kind of transparency to the moral, so that it is more easily perceived.

The manner in which a fable is narrated is also a vital element in its success or failure. In the 1779 set, Krasicki achieves a high degree of intensity with which his contemporaries in Augustan Poland were unable to compete. The fables of Naruszewicz, in contrast, have faded and retain little more than antiquarian interest.

I *The Parables*

Krasicki's title (*Fables and Parables*) indicates that the collection includes a number of "parables." As used in the New Testament, parables are short tales that enable the hearer or reader to grasp a meaning without any direct explanation by the teller. Usually, too, the truths parables illustrate are more noble and elevated than the morals demonstrated by fables. The characters who participate in parables are human beings, though the humans are usually of a general type: a hypocrite, a philosopher, a bigot, a miser. Alternatively, they may be representatives of a group: a doctor, a servant, a shepherd. Krasicki's consistent use of these general types demonstrates yet again that he was primarily inter-

ested in Mankind, viewed as a collection of "types," and less concerned with individuals. This attitude recurs in his satires, where
he deals with types such as the Fashionable Wife, the Drunkard
and the Miser, and again in his novels, which are populated by
representative types of humanity.

Like the fables, Krasicki's parables are marked by economy of
means. Economy and brevity were Krasicki's cardinal principles
in both kinds of stories, which rarely exceed eight or ten lines.
Usually he prefers to condense his meaning into four or six lines.
Working in such brief compass means, of course, that every word
must be made to work to the utmost. Not a word can be wasted,
or used merely for ornament or to provide a rhyme. When an
adjective appears, for example, it is made to serve a specific purpose—when Krasicki remarks that a certain sheep was "fat" (I,
13), the attribute is certain to have an essential bearing on the
sheep's character and fate, and therefore on what the fable is
about. This particular sheep is represented as "vain" about his fat-
ness (though without knowing why). Too late, the sheep discovers he is being fattened for a sacrifice, and is ceremoniously
slaughtered despite his "wreaths and gilded horns."

Epithets also point and heighten contrasts, or underline a basic
antithesis between two characters taking part in an argument.
Antithetic characters include an "old" and a "young" fox, a "mis-
serly" father and "extravagant" son, a "valuable" diamond and
"worthless" crystal.

As the late Professor Kleiner showed in his enlightening study
of Krasicki's fables,[3] antithesis provides the structural pattern for
almost all the fables and parables of the 1779 set. Time and again,
Krasicki illustrates a conflict, based on contrary interests, or on the
divergence between spiritual and material values. The basic antithesis to which he frequently returns is that between truth and
falsehood, or what might now be called the disparity between
"reality" and "illusion" that informs innumerable poems, plays and
novels in European literature. The conflict is the basic theme of
works in Polish as apparently unlike as Mickiewicz's *Pan Tadeusz*
(1834),[4] and *Lalka* (The Doll, 1890) by Boleslaw Prus.

Krasicki underlines the magnitude of the contrast or disparity
by examining it in different contexts, and in terms of different
situations. A young fox, blissfully "ignorant of the hunter's trade,"
delights in the appearance of his winter coat—only to be re-

minded that the fur will be the cause of his death (I, 4). A rat, sitting on an altar, thinks incense is being burned in his honor: stifled by the smoke, he falls victim to a predatory cat (I, 8). A mouse who has eaten a "whole book" assumes she now possesses "all knowledge," and offers to make away with the cat. The latter slyly agrees to listen to the mouse's argument. "The cat listened attentively/Sighed and wept . . . The mouse, seeing she'd won him over/Fell deeper into rhetorical fervor,/Came out of her hole —and then the cat got her" (I, 20).

The process of disillusion is not always as dramatic or catastrophic as it was for the fox, the rat or the mouse: a little stream envies the "impetuous waters enormously roaring" in a fountain. But the fountain's pipes burst, and the stream realizes with "inexpressible delight," that "Art never rivals Nature." Art, being an illusion, must yield to Nature (i.e. to Truth) (II, 6). A philosophical cat complains that although she catches mice for her master, he is not her "true friend," whereupon he reminds her that she catches mice not for his sake, nor for the sake of friendship, but "because mice are tasty" (IV, 21). The theme is treated in one of the best-known of all Krasicki's fables:

> A young finch asked an old one why he wept:
> "There's comfort in this cage where we are kept."
> "You who were born here may well think that's so—
> But I knew freedom once, and weep to know." [5]

Another kind of contrast appears in the way Krasicki provides examples of theory and practice: a lion invites other animals to accompany him on a hunting expedition, so that he may display his magnanimity. But on seizing his prey, the lion devours the meat, and leaves only bones for the other animals. Once his benevolence has brought him celebrity, the lion magnanimously gives the other animals permission—to eat one another. Then, to set an example, the lion decides it is only right that he should eat all the rest himself (I, 26).

A wolf enters into an alliance with the sheep: one day a lamb is devoured, and the "sheep set up an outcry." But to this the wolf replies: "Why complain?/Our treaty makes no mention of lambs." Later, the wolf cannot resist devouring a sheep, protesting: "She offered herself to be caught." Still later, he slays several more sheep, but is able to find excuses for his behavior: finally he devours the entire flock (III, 11). A pious lady, vexed by her servant-girl as she herself was ending a prayer, turned to the girl saying "Forgive us our trespasses, as we forgive them that trespass against us"—and beats the poor girl mercilessly (III, 6).

II *The* New Fables

The fable was Krasicki's preferred poetic genre. As he declared, "Witty fables are the most perfect aim of poetry," and he returned to them throughout his career. A second set, entitled *New Fables,* was published posthumously in 1802. This collection differs from the earlier set in that Krasicki allowed himself considerably more freedom in developing his narratives, in the use of dialogue and in artful characterization.

Now, too, he abandons for the most part the regular, end-stopped couplets with lines of equal length, and turns instead to the irregular lines used by La Fontaine and the eighteenth-century fabulists, most of whom were unable to match the hard brilliance of the Augustan couplet. In the *New Fables,* lines vary from ten or eleven syllables to only two or three. Such irregularity in the versification was permissible in low genres like the fable, and Krasicki may well have expressed his preference for the genre precisely because fables offered greater freedom in subject-matter and form than did the elevated genres, such as tragedy and epic—both of which he attempted, though with marked lack of success. A characteristic feature of the eighteenth-century poetry that continues to live today, is the poetry in low genres, where "rules" were not applied too rigidly. In these kinds of poetry, writers could give reign to imagination and fantasy.

"The Owls" (I,6) shows Krasicki's skill in characterizing his creatures:

> Madame Owl, worthy of her spouse
> Hence prolific,
> Bore six owlkins, and some owl-lets too;

Proud of her "daughter, son, grandchildren" Madame Owl encourages them to fly about, but sighs that "in my time, everything went better," at which the "youngest owlkin, favorite of Madame Owl" pipes up:

"No sooner did we fly out (of the "hole in the chimney" where the owls live)

> Than all the other birds fell silent,
> They all squeezed into corners,
> Not one dared utter a sound:
> Only we owlkins soared up.
> Some little birdlet in a bush,
> Of the kind they call a nightingale,
> Was giving forth a mournful cry;
> But even he dared not mutter
> As soon as we started to hoot."

Gratified by the success of her offspring, Madame Owl nevertheless feels it necessary to provide them with "spiritual food," and declares:

> "Though your voice be fine, your flight so extensive,
> Learn, dear infants, to be humble too.
> It is fitting we forgive the frailty of others:
> Not everyone is called upon by God to be an owl."

Unfortunately, the present writer's limited resources cannot render Krasicki's *tone* in this fable—achieved partly through the easy colloquialness of language, diminutives, sudden drops into bathos ("Having soared their full,/They returned to their abode,/That is, a hole in the chimney") and the rhymes.

We are fortunate in having one of the *New Fables* successfully translated into an English version which retains Krasicki's meter and rhyme system: in "The Heron, the Fish and the Crabs," Krasicki blends neat characterization and fast-moving narrative to make his moral point:

> A heron growing old, as they often do,
> A little blind, and crooked too,
> So, when she couldn't catch another fish,
>   Thought of a ruse to fill her empty dish.
>   She said to the fish: "You cannot know
>   Why I am weeping so."
>   So they asked her to tell,
>   And listened well.
>   "Yesterday,

                I heard them say,
            The fishermen who work
            Here by day and by dark,
            That they were weary
            Of their labor dreary,
        'Let's empty the pond and take the lot,
    There's not much they can do when the pond's dry, but rot.' "
            The fish wept, and the heron sedate,
            Said: "I pity your fate.
            There's but one thing you must do.
            Another pond lies nearby,
            Which they will never dry.
            Make that your home. Go there!
            Fly through the splendid air."
            "O take us!" cried the fish,
            But the heron didn't wish
            To help them, and gave way
            Reluctantly to their plea.
    One at a time she flew off with them in her beak,
            And swallowed them without a squeak.
    Bloated with fish, she fancied some crabs.
            One, scenting treachery, grabs
    Her by the neck as she flies over the ground,
            And so she perishes without a sound.
                And so all sly
                Traitors die.[6]

From this sample, it is apparent that although Krasicki's manner of narrating has changed, the fables are still taking place in a
world when treachery and cunning triumph over the innocent and
trusting. Another of the *New Fables* ("The Friends") makes the
point still more clearly: a young rabbit gambolling in the fields
and gardens is so "very pretty, delightful and sweet" that all the
other animals loved him, and he in turn was a friend to them
all—until "alarming voices of hunting-horns, barking of hounds
and a great uproar" are heard. In flight, the rabbit begs help from
his "friends"—the horse assures him "others" will assist him escape
the hunters, the bull suggests he hide in the grass or turn to the
goat, who recommends him to seek the sheep's aid. The sheep
tells him to appeal to the calf, who declines to help "because all
the others have refused." Finally, "As all means of rescue came to

naught,/Amidst his sincere friends, the dogs ate the rabbit"
(II, 9).

III *Variety*

The two sets of fables together contain some two hundred examples of the difficult yet rewarding genre, and Krasicki gives
ample evidence throughout of his extraordinary skill in introducing variety into a literary kind which—in the hands of a less
skilled practitioner—might easily have declined into monotony.
Krasicki makes his satirical points in several ways: sometimes he
speaks in his own "voice," as in the introductory fable already
quoted (p. 43), and in *Marriage* (II, 15):

> Thank Heaven! A marriage like we knew of old,
> A harmony of spirits in one mould,
> Whose love was lasting and beyond all praise.
> Too bad! The groom lived only seven days.[7]

Elsewhere, however, we hear only the voices of his characters,
arguing, disputing, quarrelling or making the point themselves, as
in *The Turtle and the Mouse* (IV, 4):

> "Shut in your cage, uncomfortable too!"
> The mouse reproached the turtle. "As for you,"
> The turtle answered, "keep your mansion fine
> And grand! My shell is narrow, but it's mine." [8]

Throughout both sets, Krasicki is displaying—with the urbanity,
grace and wit that characterize all his writing—his penetrating
knowledge of, and sympathy for, the frailties of his fellow-man.

CHAPTER 5

The Polish Socrates

WHILE Krasicki was writing the fables (which took as their subject what may be called "general" follies and vices), he was also composing his first set of twelve satires (directed against the follies and vices of contemporary society).

Dr. Johnson defined satire as "poems in which wickedness or folly are censured," and this is the function of Krasicki's volume of satires published in Warsaw in 1779, with a second volume containing eight examples of the genre, published in 1783. As usual, Krasicki makes clear thus his allegiance to Horace, who also published two sets of satires (ten in 35 B.C., and eight in 30 B.C.): and like Horace, Krasicki uses satire to express close involvement with the society of his own day on the one hand, and his revulsion from certain of its manifestations on the other.

Satire was particularly well-suited to eighteenth-century minds, for it was an age when poets, philosophers and scientists were subjecting the human species to close examination. This was a time when cultivated society was still comparatively small and a need was generally felt for order and conformity—especially after the disorders of the previous age. Consequently ladies and gentlemen of fashion all over Europe scrutinized one another's conduct, and sought anxiously to avoid departing in any way from accepted standards of conduct or thought. Fortunately, they were unaware of the violent dislocations that the French Revolution would bring to their carefully ordered society (typified by the extraordinary home lives of Romantics like Byron or Mickiewicz, for example).

Satire had respectable literary antecedents, and this in itself—as we have already seen—was always a recommendation to Augustan poets. The genre had flourished under the Emperor Augustus in Imperial Rome, when writers employed it as a persuasive art to restore balance to society, and to correct the errors of men's ways by working on their minds with words. Whether satire ever reformed anyone is at best doubtful, and it would be vain to inquire if Horace cured any misers of avarice, or if Juvenal purified the morals of a single Roman. Even so, satire in one form or another has always been enjoyed by those of us who apply it, not to ourselves, but to other people.

Krasicki was not by any means the first Polish poet to use satire as an instrument of moral, social or political reform. Various kinds of satire had flourished from the sixteenth century onwards, and Krasicki's contemporary, Adam Naruszewicz had published a set of his own satires (totalling the Horatian eight) the preceding year (1778). In their own day, the fame of Naruszewicz as a poet outshone that of Krasicki, though posterity has reversed this judgment, and his satires do not bear comparison with those of the latter.[1]

Krasicki's satires differ in one respect from much eighteenth-century satire, in that Krasicki—unlike the authors of the many satirical lampoons that flourished in Warsaw as in London and Paris—avoids making personal attacks on recognizable people. The "invective satire" practiced by Alexander Pope in his *Dunciad*, for instance, where he derides and attacks persons his readers could (and did) identify, was written and circulated in eighteenth-century Warsaw. But Krasicki went to some pains to assure a friend, before his satires appeared in print, that they "do not call anybody by name, so that the public need not be alarmed." The personages that populate his satires are representative types, not individuals, although Krasicki succeeds in endowing the types with life.

As Krasicki well knew, literary theory since classical antiquity had recognized three kinds of verse satire, and his two collections contain examples of each. His concern with alternating the forms, and providing variety by doing so, is as inconspicuously present here as it was in the fables.

The recognized forms were the "sermon," in which the satirist speaks, as it were, in his own voice, addressing the reader directly. He relies, like a skilful preacher, on changes of tone to hold the reader's attention as he examines a human vice or folly, turning it around to expose as many aspects as possible. The second form is the "portrait gallery" satire, in which the satirist parades several wicked, deluded, vain or benighted creatures for inspection, and comments on their faults. The third form is the quasi-dramatic "conversation piece," of which Horace's Satire I, 9 ("The Bore") is the classical example. In this kind, the satirist presents a narrator (who may or may not speak for the satirist), and his interlocutor (the "adversarius"): the latter's function is to ask leading questions of the narrator, and to elicit all kinds of information about the narrator—or, alternatively, to reveal himself through irrational, foolish or wicked behavior.

On occasion, the narrator himself asks the questions, and here the classical model occurs in the Dialogues of Plato, where Socrates is shown ironically eliciting answers to questions that seem easy, but which are so phrased that the replies of the other speaker are manifestly absurd. Krasicki was highly successful in this role, and his literary resemblance to Socrates is heightened by a deliberate refusal to state any moral or philosophical truths while playing the part. Krasicki intends his readers—as Plato had done—to criticize the foolish speaker whom he has exposed, by the exercise of our own rational faculties.

Throughout his satires, Krasicki is operating in accordance with well-defined (though usually unstated) standards of what is right or wrong, good or bad, proper or improper. Generally speaking, however, the representative types in the satires have sinned against Reason, rather than against moral or theological laws.

In addition to being Horatian in form (as just mentioned), Krasicki's satires are also Horatian in spirit. Very rarely does Krasicki give voice to anything resembling the uncompromising venom and indignation of Juvenal. Like Horace, Krasicki much prefers the role of teacher, and most of his targets, too, are in essence vices of the royal court: envy, hypocrisy, ambition, flattery. He sets out to edify through satire, and does so in an easy, urbane and often conversational tone that is suggestive of sophisticated intellect.

Can satire be considered "poetry"? It *is* poetry—by eighteenth-century standards, and in any case, satire has always provided lively minds with opportunities to study and comment upon human nature, and to reflect contemporary life. There is poetry of a special kind in the artistry of satirists like Horace, Pope and Krasicki, achieved largely by their use of language. Being a "low" genre, satire did not need the artificial respiration of poetic diction, and this in turn meant that it admitted, and indeed encouraged the introduction of colloquial language, a distillation—as it were—of the language spoken by cultivated society in the drawing-rooms, coffee-houses and at the royal court in Warsaw.

The art of the satirist is made manifest chiefly in his choice and placing of words, in his handling of rhyme, caesura and similar "technical" devices.

I Vices and Follies

Following closely in the footsteps of Horace, who exalted the Emperor Augustus in poetry as the representative of an ideal monarch, Krasicki begins his first set of satires with one addressed to the King. However, this is by no means a typical eighteenth-century panegyric, of the kind composed by Naruszewicz and lesser writers, flattering Stanislas Augustus for virtues he never possessed. On the contrary, Krasicki's satire to the King is marked by deliberate ambiguity, and the reader's task is to decide when Krasicki is speaking seriously, and when ironically. But he does not go as far as Pope who, in his rendering of Horace's *Epistles* II, 1 (addressed to the Emperor Augustus), permitted himself a tone that was exclusively ironical, even sarcastic.

Pope's "Advertisement" to the "Horatian Epistle" ends on a note that is relevant to Krasicki's satire. He said: "We may further learn from this Epistle, that Horace made his Court to this Great Prince by writing with a decent Freedom toward him, with a just Contempt of his low Flatterers, and with a manly Regard to his own Character."

Krasicki too displays a "manly Regard to his own Character," and warns his august reader that "Satire speaks the truth, makes no allowances:/ It admires the office, honors the king, but judges the man." Krasicki does not hesitate to declare that the king has several faults: although Stanislas is the king, he is not the son of a king, and "this is bad." Following Polish traditions (which knew no hereditary monarchy), Stanislas had been elected by an assembly of the Polish gentry, and the fact that he was not of royal blood was held against him by the ultra-conservatives among the gentry. But Krasicki's complaint against royalty is based on other objections: "royalty breathe different air, live on different foods" from the rest of humanity, and are therefore "wise without needing to learn, proficient without having to work." Everything comes easily to monarchs, they are "naturally virtuous, naturally respected" by later generations, and poets "naturally" sing their praises. That, Krasicki remarks, is what poets are for.

From here it is but a step to Krasicki's next complaint: "You are a king, why aren't I?" He too has worthy attributes: he is well-born and, above all, he too is a Pole. Reverting to the king's unpopularity among the reactionary gentry, Krasicki now chides them for praising the king outwardly, while refusing to honor him in their hearts. For a moment Krasicki appears to be in agreement with them: "After all, in Lacedaemonia/ A Thessalian always sat on the throne,/ The Romans summoned their dictators from the Greeks," on the principle that "It was always better when foreigners ruled." Consequently, even the fact that Stanislas was himself a Pole can be held against him.

Another grave fault in the king (Krasicki continues) is that he is "young." Stanislas, who was thirty-two at the time of his election in 1764, has "neither grey hair, nor wrinkles," though it is only by acquiring them that a man can be said to possess "talents and wisdom." Krasicki blandly expresses the hope that Stanislas will improve in these respects, adding: "As soon as we see you in decrepit old age,/We shall complain—because you are old."

Krasicki's next "complaint" is directed against the king's method of ruling, and he inquires: "Why have friends? Let your servants admire you. Let them fear you." The king's taste for books and the company of rational persons has its share of disapproval: "No nation was ever made powerful by a book," and Krasicki refers as evidence to the legendary King Wizimierz, who "captured the Danish fleet, though he was unable to read or write."

Krasicki proceeds to demonstrate that "It is not necessary, your majesty, to have a kind heart." The very fact that Stanislas is benevolent and kind-hearted (as opposed to the tyrannous despots Frederick the Great and the Empress Catherine of Russia, for example) only serves to vex his subjects, including the satirist himself. His advice to the king, therefore, is "Be wicked; then, by counterbalancing your virtues,/ I will praise you—when you improve."

Throughout the 120 lines of this satire (which Stanislas studied carefully before it was published), Krasicki is turning inside-out the fashionable panegyrics that flourished in the Augustan period. By voicing the complaints of the discontented gentry—who indeed attempted to dethrone the king in 1768—in such a way as to

expose their irrelevance, Krasicki discreetly signals to his readers
that the satire means the opposite of what he is saying.

The first satire proper is "The World Decay'd," which is a vigor-
ous denunciation of contemporary Polish society, with outbursts
of righteous indignation expressed in frequent exclamations, rhetorical questions and apostrophes. Polish society, as Krasicki sees
it, is in a deplorable state, with "sophistry and lying," "unbelief,"
"Godless books" abounding. Wherever he looks, the satirist sees
"disorder, depravity and shameful crimes," as the "Godless rabble
blindly rushes into an abyss of folly" like so many Gadarene
swine.

He calls in vain on the spirits of Poland's forebears to glance
down upon the earth—though he doubts whether they will recognize their descendants, for "we are profligates, unworthy of the
name of Poles." As this passage indicates, the satirist is so appalled
by the "world decay'd," that he includes himself in the castigation.

Dismayed by the vices and follies he sees all around him, Krasicki utters a solemn warning, reminding his readers that "Virtuous
Rome was victorious—criminal Rome perished./ It was not the
Goths and Huns that reduced Rome utterly,/ But her own
crimes."

The second satire, "Malice Conceal'd and Open," offers living
examples of the vices Krasicki sees everywhere. His first choice in
the portrait gallery, selected at random in the "throng of tricksters
and cheats" is a certain Wojciech, a man treacherous and sly by
nature, but who succeeds in keeping his treachery concealed from
sight. When Wojciech betrays or tricks someone, he rejoices—but
in secret. Other people's misfortunes are an agreeable spectacle to
be relished. Indeed, his "favorite beverage" consists of the tears he
causes other people to shed, while "an insincere smile flits across
his face,/ In his eyes a spark of rancor glitters and burns." But
Krasicki reassures us in an aside that "Treachery will expose itself
in time,/ The mask will fall, and the traitor beneath,/ Be all the
more repulsive, the longer he was hid."

Wojciech is followed by Konstanty, who also has the skill of
artfully concealing his treacherous acts, so that his victims often
fall into his trap without realizing it. Outraged, the satirist cries:
"Where now is honesty?" Rome is invoked again, and a contrast
with Warsaw implied, as Krasicki reminds us "Rome had her
Verres, her Cataline, and her Cato." But now eighteenth-century

Warsaw cannot show even a single noble patriot, and even Honesty has learned to be compliant for the sake of profit. When circumstances permit, the most respectable and honest men will thieve and betray their fellow-men—though they will do so in an agreeable, elegant, charming manner. Konstanty is an example of the typical eighteenth-century "gallant," as the species was depicted in Restoration comedy on the English stage. Polish literature of the age also abounds in portraits of "gallants," and Krasicki offers other specimens in his novel *Nicholas Find-Out* (1785).

Next in the portrait gallery comes Pawel, who has "attended mass thrice, said four rosaries, joined all the brotherhoods . . . and lends out money in usury." The moneylender, charging exorbitant rates of interest, was a familiar figure of scorn and derision in eighteenth-century Europe: Pope attacked usurers by name in the *Moral Essays*, while in Russia Catherine tried to stamp out the practice by means of legislation, and usurers were satirized on the St. Petersburg stage in comedies.

After expressing his horror of such hypocritical pharisees as Pawel, Krasicki addresses him directly, warning he may "trick people, but will never cheat God." The parade continues with another hypocrite, the free-thinker Jedrzej, who has "thrown aside the respectable veil of Virtue and Shame," to become "leader of the Ungodly." On his table lie the works of "sinful blasphemers," and although Krasicki does not name these writers, they no doubt included Voltaire, Rousseau and other French "philosophes." Needless to say, Krasicki himself read their works, but the point he is making in this satire is that Jedrzej puts them to wrong uses. In any case, the satirist should not be taken to represent Krasicki himself: like most eighteenth-century writers, Krasicki more often than not adopts a mask, from behind which he speaks as though he were another person, with other standards and beliefs. The sight of the books is too much for the satirist, who exclaims "Let us turn away our eyes,/ We have had too many of such regrettable scenes."

But he has not yet reached the end of the parade: next appears "proud Jan," boasting his noble ancestry and high birth, which give him the right to do as he pleases. He believes his title puts both sense and virtue in the shade, so "he takes his stand, and despises all the world." Similarly, wealthy Michael thinks his money gives him the right to deride enlightened men for being poor. But we are advised not to inquire too deeply into the source of Michael's wealth: "Did he steal it, or obtain it by fraud? Suffice that he has it."

Piotr is the next example, and Krasicki explains that Piotr holds his position in Warsaw society by flattery and the adroit use of pleasing compliments, though he himself has neither money nor property. In contrast to Piotr is Franciszek, an "alchemist," another species that flourished in eighteenth-century Europe, especially Russia.[2] An example was the notorious charlatan Cagliostro, who visited both St. Petersburg and Warsaw in the 1770's, and used his knowledge of "alchemy" to defraud credulous persons. Krasicki's example is seeking the philosopher's stone which will enable him to transmute base metals into gold. He "sits by his little stove" and "puffs the coals," surrounded by cupboards full of chemicals, retorts and other apparatus. Catching sight of a spark in the fire, Franciszek deludes himself into believing he has been successful at last. But the satirist knows better: "I congratulate but cannot envy him . . . Even though he were to manufacture gold, he has already lost his all."

The moralist steps forward to conclude this satire, and to remind of the not very original truth that "Gold does not make for happiness . . . The foundation of all is honesty, piety and virtue." To stress the practical significance of what we have been shown, Krasicki adds: "Let us change our ways and set to work,/ Let Poles be virtuous, and they will be happy." This patriotic note will be heard again in later satires and the *Epistles*.

II *Two Voices*

Satire III, "The Good Fortune of Tricksters," introduces a new form, which Krasicki uses successfully in several later pieces. This is a dialogue between two persons, the satirist (as narrator), and his interlocutor, a figure whose role is confined to asking questions which the narrator is pleased to answer.

It is New Year, and the time for compliments: first, the satirist considers Jedrzej, who has spent the Old Year "seeking where to worm his way in, or gain some profit" with his venal tongue, and Szymon, a "lover of humankind," who is nevertheless perfectly prepared to praise wicked and good indiscriminately, and who measures virtue and vice by the same standards.

After considering Jedrzej and Szymon, the satirist decides he has no intention of complimenting such men as they, whereupon his interlocutor points out: "No, you are wrong," for all men are not alike. The satirist has to admit this, and agrees that there are virtuous men and women in the world—though not many of them. He now turns his attention to those persons of his acquaintance for whom the Old Year was fortunate, and whom "Fate endowed with everything their hearts desired." They include Konstanty, with his "bold look and brazen forehead," who treads a "flowery path," and whom Good Fortune watches over— even while he sleeps. The din of flattery surrounds him, and he has the power of hearing only that which is agreeable: he is deaf to reproach.

The satirist decides he has reason to compliment Paul. A year ago, Paul was having to count pennies, but now he "counts them by the thousand." Piotr, too, deserves an ironical compliment: he grew fat during the Old Year, and the satirist hastens to compliment Piotr's wife as well. After a glance at Wincenty, who acquired a property by fraud, the satirist attempts (rather late in the day) to console the genuinely virtuous by assuring them that "dishonesty rarely ends as it begins" and "virtue will be its own reward."

In treating the vice "Extravagance" (No. IV), Krasicki again chooses to speak through two voices, though this time neither the narrator nor the interlocutor take part in the incidents described. Their function is to discuss and comment on the two characters Wojciech and Konstanty ("generic" names). Both these characters are ruled by extravagance, and Krasicki provides their entire biographies in the course of some hundred lines. However, the biographies are presented from the viewpoint of the narrator and interlocutor, both equally detached from Wojciech and Konstanty. Yet the misspent lives of these two are not presented in the form of plain narrative. Instead, Krasicki introduces the element of time, and makes it a structural part of the satire. He dwells inconspicuously, yet pointedly, on the inter-relation between present and past time.

Wojciech's past life is compared to his present by means of temporal adverbs: "Did you know Wojciech previously?" "Who didn't? He who now/Without servants, flounders in the mud . . . Formerly he pouted and ogled in his carriage,/ Which jostled and spattered such as he is today." But "those carefree days did not last long." His boon companions, gallants, toadies, seeing Wojciech ruined by squandering his money on "greedy desires," soon deserted him. "Poverty remained, and with it, shame of his former pride." Now, instead of quenching his thirst with champagne, he does so at the well. Krasicki, with his characteristic economy, tells the tale of Wojciech in twenty lines, by contrasting his past wealth and present poverty.

Konstanty, the other example of extravagance at its worst, is dealt with at considerably greater length (lines 25–124). The first section shows him against the background of his ancestral home, the walls hung with family portraits, the rooms full of old furniture, faithful retainers abound, and the cellars are well stocked with wine laid down by his grandfathers. We next see Konstanty in the framework of a typical day (lines 71–102), where the time element is made clear: "As soon as day breaks, there's barely room to move in the vestibules . . . Parrots caw in cages, goldfinches chirrup, . . . the clock plays a tune every fifteen minutes, and on the hour."

Time continues to fly past as Konstanty replaces all the old furniture with new, purchases "two alleged Van Dykes and four Rubens" (although as Konstanty informs his admiring friends, Rubens was best as a sculptor and Van Dyke as an architect). Meanwhile, however, the estate is going from bad to worse, his agents and clerks defraud and cheat him on all sides.

Konstanty decides to make the fashionable Grand Tour of Europe, with which wealthy young men finished off their education in the eighteenth century. The doubtful value of such trips had already been exposed in the *Monitor*, where, in 1767, the fictitious "diary" of a fashionable young gallant had shown him preoccupied by eating, drinking, playing cards, having his hair cut, reading novels and getting into debt. Krasicki returned to the theme of a foolish young man travelling in Western Europe in the novel *Nicholas Find-Out*.

While Konstanty is away, his agent at home continues to defraud him, forging documents, selling and, entering into worthless mortgages, signing promissory notes—until Konstanty returns to find he is nothing but a "fashionable pauper," just in time for the narrator (who has been giving an account of what happened to

Konstanty in his own words) to deliver his moral and point the satire: "Extravagance, which glories in mere empty appearance,/ Adorns outwardly, but in reality is destructive."

The use of time as a structural element in this satire is connected with the vice extravagance, a human failing with long-term effects on the characters of both Wojciech and Konstanty. Its baleful influence could not have been illustrated with the same dramatic effect in the "portrait gallery" type of satire which preceded "Extravagance." Time itself was necessary for the extravagance of Wojciech and Konstanty to show its workings. The care with which Krasicki's narrator establishes Konstanty's downfall in its temporal sequence adds an additional dimension to his portrayal.

From "Extravagance" Krasicki next turns his attention to its opposite, in "Miserliness" (V). This time, Krasicki's narrator is provided with an interlocutor named Alexis, who asks a series of leading questions. But first of all, Krasicki's narrator gives a rapid portrait of his typical miser, wearing a "torn coat," as he sits down to breakfast on a scrap of yesterday's warmed up meat, while he has quantities of gold locked away in an oak chest.

Alexis is curious to know the source of the miser's wealth: did he find a treasure, or did his late wife leave him a fortune? Did he win a law-suit? Or was it an alchemist who made the gold for him? No, it was none of these: the miser gained his fortune because he was an expert in "pennies," and as the satirist points out, great things can come from small beginnings. "From hoarding brass coins, you aspire to silver coins, and thence to gold."

Krasicki proceeds to illustrate this somewhat unoriginal moral by introducing the figure of Piotr, who—for all his efforts—did not observe the principle, and rapidly found himself in debt and bankrupt. Alexis inquires: "Was he extravagant?"/"No," says the narrator, "he lived wretchedly, never invited guests." "Perhaps his wife was to blame?" asks Alexis. "No, she sat at home spinning, feeding the poultry and baking." Mystified (as, of course, the narrator intended him to be), Alexis is forced to inquire: "So—what brought about his losses?" The reply, to which the narrator has been carefully leading up, is simply that Piotr was not an expert in "pennies"—he squandered them needlessly, but when the "pennies" were added up, they amounted to a considerable sum.

III *Self-Revelation*

Satire VI deals with a failing notoriously widespread in the eighteenth century—drunkenness. Structurally, this satire differs from the others in this set, in that the narrator himself is the object of Krasicki's satire. His narrative is so devised that he reveals his own character by what he says and does. His first words, in answer to the interlocutor's neutral question "Where are you off to?" provide an insight into his failing as he protests: "I can scarcely walk . . . You know I never overdo drinking, but my head is aching so . . ."

The drunkard's tale, which constitutes over two-thirds of this satire, is in effect a monologue set inside the framework of the narrator-interlocutor dialogue. He describes three separate incidents which, when taken together, have reduced him to his present condition: first, his wife's birthday celebration "the day before yesterday," which lasted until dawn. This was followed by the drunkard's awakening "at noon," suffering from a headache, for which he sought various remedies (his wife suggested tea, but he rejected that beverage as "insipid"). The final incident "yesterday" was the arrival of two boon-companions from the previous day's debauch, leading to more strong drink and the climax—a brawl.

The brawl is treated at greater length than the two preceding happenings, and the drunkard presents it as a dramatized scene, with dialogue. The three boon-companions soon become involved in a political argument—while the bottles gradually empty on the table. By the time they reach the tenth, Jedrzej bursts into maudlin tears. The narrator tries to pacify them, but now has to admit he cannot recall how the quarrel ended, except that someone hit him on the head with a bottle.

By this time, the drunkard has revealed a good deal of his own character and the effect his vice has upon it. From the direct revelation in his narrative, he passes to indirect revelation as he exclaims: "Perdition take disgusting drunkenness! What's the good of it? Nothing but sickness, quarrelling and brutality . . . Nausea, bruises and sticking-plaster." Krasicki has almost made his satirical point, though not quite. He reserves his final touch in the portrait of the drunkard until the last line. In the meantime, the drunkard's interlocutor reappears, and comments in a series of moralizing aphorisms on the unedifying narrative: "You speak well—'tis the diversion of low boors,/ A respectable man loathes drunkenness as a vile thing;/ From it come quarrels and unseemly scandals . . . It ruins health and shortens life . . ." Clearly this is one of the occasions when it is more than the satirist's moral duty to speak his mind—it is a pleasure. Krasicki endows his interlocutor with a strong dose of self-satisfaction and he continues in this moralizing vein for over twenty lines.

Finally the drunkard interrupts the sermon with an abrupt: "Goodbye!" The interlocutor pauses momentarily in his flow of well-intentioned eloquence to ask: "Where are you off to?" and the drunkard's final, curt "To drink a vodka" instantly deflates the sermonizing. The drunkard has exposed himself as unable to acknowledge the error of his ways, and lacking the capacity even to understand. But this attitude accords precisely with what we already know of his character.

"Drunkenness" is an eminently Horatian satire, in that Krasicki constructs it in the form of a dramatic dialogue, and makes the interlocutor merely a secondary figure. For all the latter's moralizing about the "vileness" of strong drink, it is not he who makes the satirical point, but the reader himself, by exercising his own rational insight.

By casting this satire in the form of a dialogue, Krasicki avoids intruding into the narrative—so that "Drunkenness" is formally close to the directness of the *Fables and Parables*, where we rarely hear the author's voice, but are persuaded to use our own reasoning powers to find out the author's true meaning. There is considerable technical skill in the way Krasicki succeeds in the portrayal of his drunkard without the use of any digressions, stage-directions (even "he said" and other such indications are absent), or comment.

The satirist adopts the appropriate role of mentor in no. VII, "Warning to a Young Man," which is in effect advice to Jan, about to enter into "the world." From what we already know of Krasicki's view of "the world," it is hardly surprising that this advice can be summed up in two words: "Be careful!" Jan will be surrounded by thieves, traitors and cheats, and Krasicki parades before his innocent listener figures such as Paul, "a past-master and expert in the fraternity of cheats," who—for all his superficial civility—never loses an opportunity to profit from anyone who comes into contact with him.

Maciej is another character to beware of: despite his "English carriage," "French footmen" and "Negro coachman," there is a secret in Maciej's prosperity—he has abandoned virtue and honor. The satirist urges Jan to contemplate Thomas, a dreadful example of extravagance and depravity: "Enfeebled, emaciated,/ An old man at twenty: his capital gone,/ His estates, properties, palaces lost," and the "memory of irrevocable damage,/ Poisons the rest of his mournful days."

The parade continues with a warning against gallantry and the fair sex, with their "silken nets in which they entrap young men." The satirist parodies contemporary fondness for neo-classical idylls and romances as he sketches the fashionable lady Filida, jilting her lover Tyrcys in favor of someone else. All the unhappy Tyrcys can do is leap from a cliff, or sit and brood by a "curving brooklet." As Krasicki warns his young listener, this is not how love affairs end in novels, but he may expect such things to happen in real life.

Once again, the satirist insists on the necessity for caution in this world of cheating, depravity and heartless flirts and, as always, Krasicki insists that the Golden Mean should be his listener's aim. Although Jan is to beware when he enters the world, he is not to go to the extreme of becoming a misanthrope, and will find "honest-wives and old-fashioned mothers" if he looks for them.

IV   *The Fashionable Wife*

Besides being the longest of the satires, "The Fashionable Wife" is also the most complex in structure, and has long been considered one of the most successful. Krasicki employs several devices familiar in modern fiction in order to ensure that his satire produces maximum effect: like a novelist, he dramatizes his narrative throughout, manipulates a carefully designed "point of view" from which the "fashionable wife" is observed, and makes full use of the time element.

The satire opens with another of the dialogues between narrator and interlocutor. These persons use their own words, and Krasicki wastes no time in introducing them or setting the scene. The characters themselves tell us all we need to know, and the opening lines establish the character of the narrator, Piotr. The interlocutor congratulates Piotr on the latter's recent marriage, but we immediately infer, from the "coldness" with which Piotr thanks him for the compliment, that he already regrets marrying, and is sadly disillusioned with the fashionable wife he has acquired. Krasicki prepares the reader for Piotr's narrative to be colored by feelings of disillusion about the state of matrimony, and this emotional coloring adds considerably to the portrait of the wife when she appears in his narrative.

Piotr admits from the outset that he himself was chiefly to blame for marrying a "fashionable lady" at all, and his mournful "Serves me right!" runs through the satire like a refrain. Although he admits that she brought him a dowry of four villages, and was "pretty, well-bred, sensible," she was nevertheless "town-bred." Before the marriage, he regarded her as "mysterious," and "intriguing," while, like a love-sick swain, he "sighed to my Phillis."

Disillusionment came rapidly: no sooner do the happy couple come to drawing up the marriage articles, than the lady begins making demands (a French maid, and the assurance that whenever she "falls sick," she will stay "in Town," and that she shall have her own carriage and so forth). Resigned to his fate, Piotr is "enrolled in the fraternity of regretful brothers."

For the next 120 lines he dwells almost obsessively on the character of his "fashionable wife" as he describes their journey from Warsaw to his country home. First, she objects to his carriage, and he is obliged to obtain a more comfortable one. When she is finally ready to set off, she is accompanied by so many articles of finery, hat-boxes, a canary and pet cat (with kittens) that there is no room for her husband. En route, she mocks his "rustic endearments," and insists that he obtain "foreign cooks, fashionable pastrymakers" as well as an elaborate dinner-service. Before the journey is over, the lady has revealed that she can be petulant, sulky, haughty and frivolous by turns.

Worse follows: on arrival at Piotr's country house, the lady loses no time in turning the place upside-down. She alters the domestic arrangements, snubs the priest, sends carriages to Warsaw for new furniture, insists on laying out a fashionable garden with "clumps of cypresses, little streams, a kiosk here, a mosque there, a hermit's grotto and a temple dedicated to Diana," where she can "ponder o'er the misfortunes of Pamela or Heloise" (two characteristically "sentimental" heroines of the day). Surrounded by a quantity of "things," the lady comes to resemble a rococco portrait of the eighteenth century, in which human beings are shown hemmed in on all sides by gilt and ormolu furniture, so that they too take on the appearance of an "object."

Like any skilled story-teller, Piotr keeps the climax till the end, and the pace of his narrative also increases. The wife holds receptions ("while I, wretched man, sit in a corner, and mope"), and during one of these occasions, while the guests are being entertained with fireworks, a rocket sets the barn afire. Although he endeavors "in tears" to extinguish the blaze, Piotr's efforts are unavailing, and he returns to the house, only to be met by "more witticisms, fault-finding and derision" from his wife and her guests. When he ventures to protest at the extravagance of his wife's ways, she reminds him firmly that after all she brought him the four villages as dowry. Finally she insists on returning to Warsaw and Piotr concludes mournfully "It serves me right!/ What's to be done? It's no use crying, as they say, over spilt milk."

Krasicki has presented the entire satire through Piotr's own words, so that the two protagonists—the fashionable wife and her victim,—are revealed through their reactions to the various situations that arise naturally from one another. Even the inventory of the wife's personal belongings, the interior decoration, the minor characters (her relatives, who appear briefly at the signing of the marriage articles, only to mock Piotr's notion that "marriage lasts until death," the priest, servants, guests at her reception)—all are shown through the eyes of the husband-narrator.

Piotr's own attitude to his wife, which ranges from admiration of her fashionable ways, through suspicion, disillusion, contempt and resignation, makes a major contribution to the portrait of the wife, while Krasicki's skill in dramatizing is evident even in such an apparently minor detail as the way he makes as little as possible of the passages linking the various incidents. More often than not, these are omitted entirely as Piotr plunges from one incident to the next without a break.

"The Fashionable Wife" is followed by "Court Life" (IX), and here again Krasicki offers yet another variation on his method of presentation. In ordering the satires for publication, Krasicki was as careful as Horace to assure variety of subject-matter, style and method between the successive poems. By this means, he achieved subtle contrasts and avoids monotony. Such concern for order and arrangement is, of course, highly characteristic of classical art.

"Court Life" is addressed to Joachim who has spent his life "amidst the courtly throng," and is therefore an expert at its intrigues, deceptions and betrayals. When the satirist urges Joachim to reveal the secret of his success at Court, the latter declines to answer, and the satirist remarks: "You are silent—clearly you are indeed a courtier," and although he himself is "but an unpolished countryman" he answers his own question. Success at Court (he declares) depends largely on nothing more than "choice of words." Ordinary people call Piotr a thief because he has stolen, but Joachim protests: "That's true, but the phrase is too strong . . . The truth is permissible, though it must be uttered politely:/ For example 'Piotr became celebrated in a somewhat risky enterprise,'/ Or 'Piotr used what was not his.'"

Now the satirist lets us overhear a "polite conversation" conducted on this principle between Piotr and Nicholas: after complimenting one another, they begin making disparaging remarks about mutual acquaintances: Jan is a cheat, Bartholomew a cardsharp, Jedrzej a wiseacre, Vincent decidedly eccentric—and so on. The door opens, there are "a thousand bows," and the king himself enters: "all smile, all crane their necks,/ This one pushes, that nudges, the next glides forward like a serpent,/ All eager to discern whom the King will favor with a gesture." The fortunate courtier is Simon, and he in turn distributes his favors on lesser mortals —Piotr is given "half a smile," Jedrzej "a quarter of a glance" and so on, down the scale. This style of behavior is not at all to the liking of the "unpolished countryman," who brings the satire to a close with an apostrophe addressed to the freedom of the countryside, where gains are lasting, if not great. These lines serve to remind us that Krasicki himself, as already mentioned, spent some thirty years on his country estate at Heilsberg, and his visits to the royal court in Warsaw became increasingly rare.

Satire X provides a brief portrait of a newly-rich peasant who has bought himself a family coat-of-arms and invented an ancestry of gentlefolk. The newly-rich with absurd pretensions of gentility were figures of fun in the eighteenth century (and earlier), as witness Molière's "bourgeois gentilhomme" in Paris and Zagoskin's Bogatonov in St. Petersburg. However, Krasicki's satire is directed less against Maciej's pretensions than against his cruelty towards his serfs, and should be read as an attack on all gentry guilty of tyranny and inhumanity to their servants.

Before reaching the final satire, Krasicki briefly attacks the comparatively innocuous vice of card-playing and then (XII) presents his "Palinode" or recantation. This is a "program satire," in which the poet defends his art and presents his motives for composing satires at all. He surveys the great classical satirists—Horace, Juvenal, Persius—but is forced to inquire "Why write satires? To correct the world? That's an impudent undertaking," and he resolves to try no more.

Yet, as we shall see in Chapter 8, Krasicki's urge to improve and correct contemporary society was so strong, that he could not resist a further set of satires, published in 1783. In the meantime he turned to another genre, and produced Poland's first modern novel.

CHAPTER 6

Novelist

K RASICKI labored throughout his life under the illusion that he could alter human nature for the better by his pen, and this illusion was one of the reasons why he turned to the writing of fiction, even though the novel was not highly regarded as a literary genre at this time. Indeed, there was considerable uncertainty as to the difference between the novel and the "romance," a moribund and almost obsolete species, mostly translated from such French examples as Mme. de Scudéry's *Grand Cyrus*—an enormously long work full of improbable adventures, unlikely characters and insipid dialogue.[1] The "romance," which can be traced back to classical antiquity, flourished all over Europe, including Poland,[2] in the sixteenth century, but was already an anachronism when Krasicki turned to writing fiction.

Though out-dated and ridiculed by enlightened people, romances proliferated. They were regarded as pernicious because they over-emphasized "passion," thereby preventing their readers carrying out "useful duties." Conduct modeled on the behavior of characters in romances would assuredly lead to irrational, even immoral conduct, and in addition the romances were offensive to reason with their tissues of improbabilities.[3] Goldsmith went so far as to say that romances were no better than "instruments of debauchery," though it is difficult to conceive of these now unreadable and forgotten tales debauching anyone. Probably their gravest fault—also leveled against them in the eighteenth century —is their triviality.

Krasicki's purpose in writing the *Adventures of Nicholas Find-Out* was partly to counteract the pernicious effects of romances (he portrays Nicholas indulging a taste for them, with ludicrous consequences) and in addition to provide a "cure for the age." Krasicki was always a skilful judge of contemporary taste, and knew how to hit on a topic that would interest his readers—

whether they read the novel as an adventure story or as lightly veiled satire. In any case, the popularity of the novel was such that three further editions were published by 1779 and printers in Warsaw and elsewhere were sufficiently encouraged to commission and publish novels by Fielding, Goldsmith, Prévost and others. The circulation of romances declined, and in this way the development of the novel proper in Poland can be traced directly to Krasicki's *Nicholas*. In effect, Krasicki brought about the sudden forward leap that brought Polish fiction to the level of Voltaire's *Candide* and Dr. Johnson's *Rasselas*.

Krasicki was an attentive reader of the English novelists, and his *Nicholas* is related to both Defoe's *Robinson Crusoe* and Swift's *Gulliver*. Both novels were translated into Polish in 1769 and 1784 respectively, but Krasicki was not, of course, dependent on translations into Polish.

I *Characters*

Krasicki's Nicholas tells his own story in the first person, looking back from a comfortable middle-age on the adventures and follies of his youth. As he claims, he is writing his *Adventures* "not for vain praise or self-humiliation, but to warn my descendants." This artless remark sets the novel's tone, and acts as a signal that we may expect Krasicki to employ one of his favorite weapons—irony—in Nicholas's narrative.

The relationship between Nicholas on the one hand, and Gulliver and Robinson Crusoe on the other is apparent in the way they are all "outward-looking" characters, not highly individualized. The world in which such characters live is clear-cut and unambiguous, the differences between right and wrong, wisdom and folly, virtue and vice are well distinguished, even though characters may err. All the situations in which these characters are placed are designed by the novelist to illuminate moral, ethical, social and other matters, from education, manners, corruption in the Polish law-courts, foreign travel, to agriculture and "natural religion." Nicholas's adventures can usefully be considered, in effect, as a series of examples, during which Krasicki discourses satirically and ironically on topics that interested him and his contemporaries. Nicholas's tale provides a framework for these two modes.

The wide range of other characters who appear and disappear as the novel proceeds function in much the same way as Nicholas.

They are puppets directed by the novelist's all-powerful hand to
illustrate and prove his points. They are of three types: the positive virtuous characters, the negative foolish or vicious characters,
and those who are introduced for comic effect. By our standards,
perhaps, these characters lack the vitality to live apart from Krasicki's stated opinions of them: but by eighteenth-century standards, such characters were interesting precisely because they are
types in which readers could believe. The unusual, the complex,
and the abnormal were deliberately sacrificed in the interests of
plausibility and verisimilitude.

II *"The Way Things Are"*

Krasicki's liking for symmetrical arrangements, apparent in his
longer poems, is again evident in *Nicholas*. The novel consists of
three books, of which the first describes Nicholas's upbringing,
education and first steps in society. In this book, Krasicki is describing "the way things are" in eighteenth-century Poland (from
internal evidence, Nicholas's tale appears to take place in the
1760's). The second, central book is set on a Utopian island somewhere off the coast of South America, and represents "how things
ought to be," while the third seeks to explain what must be done
to better man's nature and the conditions in which he lives.

III *Education*

As befitted the Age of Reason, education was a matter that
caused a good deal of concern all over Europe. Frederick the
Great, the Empress Catherine of Russia and King Stanislas Augustus were among the representative individuals of the period
who were interested in the establishment of an improved educational system in their respective countries. But education did not
mean the mere acquisition of knowledge for its own sake: it was
regarded instead as one of the most effective means of producing
virtuous and patriotic citizens who would contribute to the better-
ment of their homeland. Krasicki shared this belief, as his statements published in the *Monitor* (1772) bear witness. He also
followed with interest the proceedings of the Educational Commission established the following year, in which the most enlightened men of their time worked to reform the principles of education and teaching.

Apart from ecclesiastical colleges conducted by the Jesuit or

Piarist orders, (which concentrated on the study of Latin grammar, classical authors, and theology), the only other means of acquiring the rudiments of an education was at home, at the hands of a tutor. However, domestic education in Poland had become a monopoly of foreigners, mostly Frenchmen or Germans, who had started making their way into Poland and Eastern Europe in the 1740's, in search of a living. The immigrants (as mentioned in Chapter 1) included men of the caliber of Mitzler de Kolof and Gröll, whose activities as printers and publishers contributed much to Poland's literary and cultural development at a time when this was urgently needed: unfortunately, however, not all the immigrants measured up to the attainments of Kolof or Gröll. Many were of dubious backgrounds, sought by the police in their own countries, poorly educated (if at all), and often unable to teach their pupils anything more valuable than a rudimentary knowledge of the French language and sketchy notions of etiquette. Russian comedies and satires of this period abound with caricatures of these persons.

Krasicki introduces a specimen of the ignorant domestic tutor into the first book of the *Adventures*. After Nicholas has conscientiously narrated his early years at home in the isolated Polish countryside, his father dies, and at this point his widowed mother engages a certain "Monsieur Damon" to be the boy's tutor. Damon is to teach him French and (more important) "good manners and presence." Damon claims he is a marquis—apparently a sufficient qualification for a domestic tutor. In any case, he assures Nicholas that "book-learning" has little or no place in his pedagogy:

Among us in Paris (he declares) the Latin language (for instance) is in such disrepute that no one who knows it can show himself in good society, ladies frown on him and gentlemen call him a pedant. Good education begins with the acquisition of presence and *ésprit*, proceeds with the forging of an elegant wit and ends with experiencing the sentiments of the heart . . .

Needless to say, these attributes can only be acquired through a knowledge of French, which Damon intends to teach to Nicholas "not by pedantic rules," but by means of "incessant conversation."

When Damon discovers that the few books which Nicholas's family own are nothing but books of devotion, he sends to Warsaw for Mme. de Scudéry's *Grand Cyrus* and *Clélie*—two of the insipid and improbable romances which Krasicki was himself deriding. Constant reading of these works produces its effect on the impressionable Nicholas, who rapidly learns to ape the outpourings of Mme. de Scudéry's Cyrus: "Permeated by elevated feelings but without any Dorinna or Clorina" (the heroines of the romances), "I sighed, complained against the gods, and would often creep into a thicket near our house, so that Echo might repeat my mournful groans."

On one such occasion, Nicholas reads a "most pathetic chapter," and is so carried away that he declaims aloud:

O why dost thou refuse to take pity on me, beloved Julianna? You prey on him who would consider himself the happiest of men, could he but be your slave . . . Command me! I am ready to venture all for thy sake, if thou wouldst but cease tormenting me so unkindly! I would betake myself to the end of the world for thee . . .

This outburst (in the best traditions of the romance) is overheard by a young orphan, ward of Nicholas's mother, who happens (by a fortunate coincidence typical of romance) to bear the name of "Julianna." Taken aback, Julianna protests: "Pray sir, do not do me that injustice! I cannot understand how deeds of mine should harm any man, let alone the son of her who is a mother to me, an orphan."

Nicholas cannot resist the temptation, and declares he has fallen in love with Julianna—much to the dismay of his mother, who considers the girl unsuitable as a wife for Nicholas, and dispatches her to a convent-school. He in turn is sent (with M. Damon) to acquire some experience and polish in "one of the leading towns in the country." He continues his adventures by being introduced by M. Damon to a certain Baroness de Grankendorff and her "daughters." Bottles of champagne and decks of cards help pass the time in the Baroness's apartment until, after several weeks, Nicholas is involved in an unseemly brawl, arrested and jailed. On his release, Nicholas finds that M. Damon has made off with all his pupil's moveable property, including his carriage, and the "Baroness" has fled too. He learns that she was nothing more than an "adventuress . . . who deceived and cheated several young men by the charms of her alleged daughters."

Nicholas's mother soon finds out what has happened, and decides that the time has come for him to go to Warsaw, where he is to reside with his uncle, a Deputy to the Polish Diet. In Warsaw, Nicholas informs us, he was able to make rapid progress thanks to advice given to him by his uncle, and, even more, from society ladies. In their company, Nicholas soon rids himself of "modesty inappropriate to a gentleman," and prides himself on his boldness and wit, which make him the "soul of elegant conversation." He is further assisted by a friend who might have stepped out of one of Krasicki's *Satires;* this individual came to Warsaw, originally, in a plain coat, without even a servant. Now he rides in an English carriage "on springs," weighted down with splendid footmen in uniform.

He confides in Nicholas that, although his family were gentry, they had been so poverty-stricken that he had been obliged to enter into service as a boy. There, he learned that his natural liveliness endeared him to those he served. He cultivated this attribute until it became effrontery. As he tells Nicholas, "He who wants to gain anything in this world must be brazen."

This is not all. Nicholas's friend expatiates on the best way to acquire the reputation in society of a "gallant," a "valiant fellow," and a "philosopher." At first, one should cultivate "effrontery, free gestures, bold talk, the art of slandering, boasting of one's own good fortune, elegant attire, a tasteful carriage, extravagant spending." To be considered a "blade," one must gain the reputation of fighting duels, and be known to keep a few pistols by one's bed ("even if they are not loaded"), and a sword in a corner of the room. As for acquiring the reputation of a philosopher ("for ours is the Age of Enlightenment") all that is needed is a few volumes by Rousseau, Voltaire and the rest in the drawing-room: "but do not think" (he adds reassuringly) "that there is any need to *read* them, or to enter into deep speculations." No, society will consider you a philosopher if you "praise what others condemn, think any way you choose, providing you do so eccentrically, make a mock of religion, take bold decisions and talk loudly."

Before Nicholas can benefit by these instructions, his mother dies: but as soon as he enters into his inheritance, he loses half at cards and is obliged to use the other half to pay off other debts. In an attempt to save the situation, Nicholas decides to sell "one or two villages" from the family estate, but finds he cannot do so without entering into a law-suit against one of his tenants. This requires a visit to the town of Lublin, location of a provincial law-court, and the episode that follows gives Krasicki the opportunity of launching a full-scale attack on corrupt judges and lawyers, as well as obsolete laws.

Krasicki had himself served as chairman of the Lublin tribunal, and knew by experience that the law-courts and legislative system of eighteenth-century Poland were in urgent need of improvement. Not that Poland was the only European country where this state of affairs prevailed: in England, Jonathan Swift had satirized the legal apparatus, while in Russia, the corruption prevalent in law-courts was one of the favorite themes of satirical playwrights, despite official disapproval.

As soon as Nicholas arrives in Lublin, he learns that a successful litigant requires three things: "Credit, or the support of powerful protectors: an acquaintance, friendship or family ties with the judges: and a lively manner which I dare not mention by name, but which equals or surpasses both friendship and family ties." The unmentionable third item is, of course, bribery. The justice or otherwise of any case is the last thing that counts.

Nicholas begins his suit by hiring a number of lawyers, and makes an excellent impression at their first conference by plying everyone with wine. He is also fortunate enough to make friends with the nephew of the President of the Court, and, finally, to procure forged documents that "prove" his ownership of the disputed property. Thus equipped, Nicholas wins his case, and decides to make a Grand Tour in Western Europe—not, needless to say, for the purpose of visiting museums and thereby broadening his mind, but as an opportunity for extravagance, profligacy and debauchery.

Krasicki now quotes from Nicholas's "Diary of my Parisian Journey" (characteristically, Nicholas's idea of Europe centers on Paris), and although the "Diary" is only three pages long, Krasicki deliberately uses a poverty-stricken style that mirrors to perfection the poverty of Nicholas's intellect. On the way, Nicholas finds time to buy expensive finery, to drink quantities of beer and wine, and to complain because the Viennese do not speak Polish. The route leads through Munich, Cologne and Strasbourg, and he reaches Paris "on February 3, at three o'clock in the afternoon."

Nicholas's extravagance makes him renowned throughout Paris. He rents a country villa for a ballet-dancer, buys quantities of clothes (discarding his home-bought finery as "out of fashion"), fashionable carriages and other items—all on credit. But this gay round of pleasure ends in disaster; his tenant has appealed against the Lublin law-court verdict, and won. Bankrupt, Nicholas decides to flee his creditors, reaches Amsterdam and is persuaded, in desperation, to sign on a ship sailing for Batavia in the East Indies.

IV *Utopia*

From a Europe populated largely by fools, liars and cheats, Nicholas is transported in the second book of the *Adventures* to the Utopian island of Nipu, where his ship is wrecked. The concept of "Utopia," in which society has become perfect, was one of the great literary metaphors of the eighteenth century, and the device whereby an author sets down his hero in a distant, usually imaginary country enabled him to provide his readers with a new look at their own society. Swift's method of proceeding in *Gulliver's Travels* is the classical example, but other writers who adopted the device to satirize the conventions, morality, constitution and social system of their own countries range from Voltaire to Samuel Butler, Anatole France and H. G. Wells.

A variation was to place a stranger from some remote country in a European setting, and in both cases, the aim was to upset the reader's usually unthinking acceptance of the manners and beliefs of his own society by reviewing them in a new light. Nicholas is so accustomed to his own society that he cannot see it as it really is until he reaches the island of Nipu and tries to describe and justify European customs and manners to the Nipuans. Only there does he achieve a modicum of detachment, and is able to see the institutions of Europe (especially Poland) with a clarity that is both instructive and devastating.

The island of Nipu, as imagined by Krasicki, bears many characteristics of the typically Utopian society. All is moderation: there are "no cripples, nor anyone very fat or very thin." The islanders wear robes "such as Greek and Roman statues wore," and there are no changes in fashion. The Nipuan language has no

words to express lying, stealing, treachery or flattery, and there
are no legal terms. Illnesses have no specific names. The Nipuans
have no courtiers, lawyers or doctors, and all are vegetarians.

When the islanders finally admit Nicholas into their society, he
decides to enlighten their ignorance and simplicity, so that they
may "imitate the European nations which outdo all others in perfection and knowledge." After a brief initiation ceremony, Nicholas is dismayed to hear his host and mentor Xaoo declare that
although Nicholas's way of thinking, speaking and acting are
harmful, yet "we must have pity on the ignorance, simplicity and
blindness of this man, who is not to blame for being born amidst
coarse and barbarous nations."

Most of Book II of the novel is taken up with the exposition of
Xaoo's opinions, and Nicholas's role is limited to that of an interlocutor in the satires. He will furnish Xaoo with a brief account of
aspects of European society, education, history, manners, philosophy and the like, and Xaoo thereupon describes at some length
the Nipuan equivalent. At first, Nicholas finds it hard to believe
that "a man who was never in Warsaw, and had never seen Paris,
could think rationally, discuss and even convince a man who has
seen and heard immeasurably more than he."

But Xaoo's views and opinions, though eminently rational, do
not convince Nicholas for long. No sooner does he find the wreck
of his ship washed up on the shore of Nipu and retrieves a large
amount of gold, bankers' orders on Paris, London and Genoa, and
several pistols, than he begins to ponder flight. Brooding in secret
on the gold, he reflects that "although the metal was of no use in
that place, the sweet memory of what it served for so inflamed my
imagination, that I could not refrain from feelings of the utmost
joy." Nicholas also retrieves a number of other articles from the
wreck, which Krasicki enumerates with all the precision of Defoe's Robinson Crusoe: they include

Spy-glasses, too damp and useless,
A sea-trumpet,
Three gold watches, one with an alarm,
A silver vase, six dishes, twelve plates,
Seven wire cages, evidently (by the feathers) once containing parrots,
A box that must have contained a wig . . .
Three broken violins, a lute, two pairs of clarinets and one trumpet,

A mahogany box with brass fittings, containing twelve flasks of lavender water.

In addition, Nicholas finds several books, which he shows to Xaoo: among them are the comedies of Molière, thirty-eight romances, four volumes of political economy, Newton's *Philosophy* (but only the third volume), and a cook-book, not to mention views of Paris. Nicholas translates the books into Nipuan for Xaoo's benefit, and the latter has this to say of Molière's *Misanthrope:*

It seems to me that the author failed to notice several things in this work of his. First, by making his misanthrope a virtuous man, he appears to suggest that virtue has within it something detestable. He deprived his virtuous misanthrope of the greatest quality of virtue— common-sense. . . . And he gave him too much self-love, by showing him flying in the face of the most commonplace customs of society.

And Xaoo concludes: "If it be not possible to avoid eccentricity without harming virtue, then I frankly admit I would prefer to be held an eccentric hermit and misanthrope, than to be fashionably dishonest."

As we shall see in chapter 8, Molière's influence on the eighteenth-century Polish theater, and on Krasicki's own plays in particular was all-pervasive.

Nicholas returns to his hidden cache of gold, and falls prey to feelings of avarice and homesickness. A conflict ensues between the dictates of his head and heart. On the one hand, he has grown accustomed to the Nipuans' "life of respectable tranquillity," and regrets his ingratitude towards his benefactors. He even resolves to throw his gold into the sea, and make a "heroic sacrifice." On the other hand, however, the sight of the gold is too much for his good intentions, and he makes his escape from Nipu in a small boat loaded with money and provisions.

His flight from Nipu comes not a moment too soon for most readers. Despite all the truth and good sense in Xaoo's utterances, and the rational, moderate way of life of the islanders, Krasicki hardly succeeds in convincing us that such a society would be even remotely tolerable if it were ever realized. The reason why these eighteenth-century Utopias (including that of Krasicki) are so unlikely, is that their authors resolutely exclude from them the one element that might have made Xaoo and the rest humanly credible—and that is the irrational aspect of human nature. The refusal to admit the existence of the irrational, the dark side of the human psyche, was a dominant feature of the age, and Krasicki was pre-eminently a man of his own time.

V *Further Adventures*

The third book of the novel, in contrast to the preceding one, abounds in incidents. Nicholas is rescued, after eleven days at sea, by a Spanish ship transporting slaves to the Bolivian mines. To Nicholas's dismay, the captain appropriates his gold, and orders him chained among the slaves. However, he has learned one lesson at least from Xaoo and the Nipauns, and resolves to endure his "cruel fate." What Xaoo's arguments had failed to convince, "the chains now persuaded." Xaoo's belief in the "cruelty of civilized nations" is proved all too apt.

On arrival at the Bolivian mines, Nicholas has the good fortune to encounter a "benevolent American," and his friend William, a Quaker, who is "one of the wealthiest merchants in Pennsylvania," who buys Nicholas out of captivity. The benevolent philanthropist was one of the stock figures in eighteenth-century didactic fiction, and Krasicki returns to the type in his *Squire* (*Pan Podstoli,* 1778–1803).

Nicholas regains his gold from the wicked captain, and sets sail for Europe. But his adventures are not yet ended: on landing in Spain, he is arrested by the Inquisition, interrogated about the island of Nipu, and immediately judged insane. Locked in a madhouse, Nicholas reflects,

In Nipu, I talked and thought like a European—they took me for a savage: in Europe, I sought to act like a Nipuan—and am taken for a madman. This reflection, placing before my eyes the oddity of my fate, imperceptibly led me to a better humor . . .

Once again, he is rescued, and makes his way home to Poland, where he is re-united with Julianna. The novel ends in a somewhat perfunctory manner with their marriage, and Nicholas settles down to a comfortable rural existence, occupied with good works, charity and virtue.

Knowing Krasicki's liking for symmetry, we may note several

parallels between books I and III: in both, Nicholas is involved in a law-suit (but in book III, which represents in part what is to be done to improve Polish society, the judges need no bribes, and the right is victorious). Similarly, the episode with Julianna in book I is echoed when Nicholas meets her again in book III.

VI *Prose Style*

In addition to being the first Polish novel in the modern sense of the word, the *Adventures of Nicholas Find-Out* is also an index to Krasicki's eminence as a stylist in prose. This is eighteenth-century prose at its most characteristic, marked by concentration and economy. The plain, unadorned language derives its effect, in the main, from Krasicki's unfailing ability to order and arrange what he has to say, so that the logical connections are immediately grasped by the reader. Each word knows its own place, and Krasicki clearly knows how each word got there.

CHAPTER 7

Fiction and History

K RASICKI'S longest imaginative work, *Pan Podstoli* (The Squire) was a resounding success when the first part was published in 1778.[1] His fame and popularity as a writer were well established in Poland by this time: even so, later works published during his lifetime were described on title-pages and in publishers' advertisements as being "By the Author of *Pan Podstoli*." The first part of the work was reprinted in 1784 (the year in which Part II appeared), and Part III was published posthumously in 1803. The last paragraphs of Part III prepare the way for yet another part, though this was never written. In any case, Krasicki spent the best part of twenty-five years working on the book.

A notion was current in the nineteenth century that the origins of *Pan Podstoli* were to be found in a planned sequel to the *Adventures of Nicholas Find-Out*, but this has been refuted.[2] A more likely source (if one is required) is to be found in the figure of Sir Roger de Coverley, from *The Spectator*—a personage Krasicki had introduced into Poland in the *Monitor*.[3] Sir Roger was one of the benevolent and philanthropic country gentlemen who populate eighteenth-century didactic fiction, and had already served as prototype of the Quaker William in *Nicholas Find-Out*. These figures express the widespread longing felt at this period for an ideal "life of moderation, composure and thoughtfulness,"[4] passed (preferably) in rural surroundings—a way of life that was, moreover, sanctioned by the examples of Horace and other classical writers.

Although *The Squire* is a work of fiction, it is hardly a novel like *Nicholas*. Many elements which we usually look for in a novel are absent: there is little characterization, and plot is lacking. To compensate, the work contains a vast deal of talk. Well-meaning attempts have been made to classify *The Squire* as a "didactic treatise in narrative form,"[5] though this in turn met with the objection that it does not have the "systematic character of a treatise." [6]

Essentially, the work looks back to a literary genre practiced during the Renaissance in Poland, as elsewhere in Europe at that time. This was the *speculum*, or "mirror," in which writers provided readers with a model for their own lives. One of the most celebrated was Baldassare Castiglione's *Cortegiano* (The Courtier), published in Venice in 1528—a book which ranks with Machiavelli's *Prince* as among the most influential books of this period. Castiglione's book was soon translated into various European languages, including Sir Thomas Hoby's English version (1561), and it reached Poland only five years later, in an adaptation by Lukasz Gornicki, significantly re-titled the *Polish Courtier* (with another edition in 1639).[7] Krasicki's Squire speaks of Gornicki's book with respect and affection (II, 11, 13).[8] Another "mirror" published in sixteenth-century Poland was Mikolaj Rej's *Proper Likeness of the Life of an Honest Man . . .* (1558), which provides a detailed picture of almost all aspects of the life of a prosperous, benevolent, pious and patriotic Polish country gentleman.

Just as the books of Gornicki and Rej had provided sixteenth-century Polish readers with pictures of somewhat idealized "courtiers" and "honest men," so Krasicki's *The Squire* was read by eighteenth-century readers as depicting an ideal way of life. The Squire's hospitable, temperate, and industrious mode of life on his prosperous country estate was one that these readers would have wished for themselves. The Squire is an example of "how things ought to be" in contemporary Poland—one of the themes of *Nicholas*.

The Polish gentry at this time was the most influential class in the Republic. The king himself, the aristocracy, and the magnates were aware of this—and, like Krasicki, they were aware that the gentry were, for the most part, still firmly rooted in the reactionary and obscurantist traditions of the Saxon past. The gentry was the class which most needed the benefits of enlightenment, and Krasicki's *Squire* was shrewdly designed to reach and appeal to this very class.

There was considerably more to the popularity of *The Squire* than this depiction of an ideal way of life, however. Krasicki provides a hint towards this other reason in the epigraph with which he furnished the book: "Moribus antiquis." In full, this motto signifies "The Roman Republic endures thanks to ancient ways and men." The motto is engraved on a beam in the Squire's dining-room, and the phrase brings Part I to a close, after the Squire has insisted at some length that "the fall of the monarchy and the republic is caused by neglect of the virtues of our eminent forbears."

Krasicki is signalizing the patriotic motives which lie behind his book, and regarded in this light, the figure of the Squire becomes a symbol of an enduring and stable way of life in a nation already a prey to internal strife and a victim to external pressures that led to the collapse and disappearance of the Polish State as an entity for longer than a century. Indeed, the process had already started when the first part of *The Squire* was published. The events leading up to the First Partition of Poland in 1772 need not be repeated here:[9] suffice it to say that by the end of that year, Poland had lost more than a quarter of her territory and four millions of her population to the partitioning powers—Russia, Prussia, and Austria. These powers later executed two further partitions (1793, 1795) which terminated Poland's existence as an independent state.

I   The Squire *and* Pan Tadeusz

Krasicki's *Complete Works* were republished in Paris in 1830, and we may suppose that this impressive one-volume edition was read by Adam Mickiewicz, the central figure of the Polish Romantic revolt, who had escaped only a year earlier from political exile in Russia to settle in Western Europe (Dresden, Paris and Rome).

Although Krasicki's *The Squire* lacks the poetic quality that makes Mickiewicz's *Pan Tadeusz* (1834) a work of great literary artistry, there is a similar atmosphere prevailing in both books, though the first is in many ways an epitome of the Age of Enlightenment, and the other an epitome of Romantic art. *Pan Tadeusz* celebrates Poland's vanished past: the action takes place in 1811–1812, when Napoleon's campaign against Russia had convinced many Poles that there was hope for the re-establishment of an independent Poland. Writing his poem twenty years later, Mickiewicz knew those hopes had been vain. Napoleon's defeat at Moscow, and the retreat of his Grand Army, only strengthened Russia's grip on the larger part of Poland which she had acquired

as a result of the three partitions. But it was precisely because
Mickiewicz knew this that he felt the urge to record a now vanished moment of time.

Life on the Squire's country estate—though separated by nearly
half a century from the way of life Mickiewicz lovingly describes
in *Pan Tadeusz*—offers a very similar picture of the "hospitality
without ostentation, ceremony without condescension, wholesome
appetite without greed," [10] to be observed on the estate of the
Judge at Soplicowo. On both estates, each with its manor, farm-
buildings, garden and surrounding landscapes, the characters live
by Horatian standards of "Temperance, Contentment and a Modest
Competence" (to quote Pope's summary of Horace's ideal). Both
estates represent an earthly paradise based on the traditions of a
society that, in Krasicki's case, were rapidly disappearing, and, in
that of Mickiewicz, had disappeared entirely.

The Squire and *Pan Tadeusz* are both, in their own ways, "realistic" works, in that they depict a range of characters, settings and
themes that are representative of a given social class at a specific
point in time (although Krasicki does not provide *The Squire* with
a definite date, there are references to Stanislas Augustus as "our
king," and the Bar Confederation (1768) is described as "recent"). Krasicki's Squire and the other characters are not exceptional or heroic individuals involved in heroic or exceptional actions: they are presented as typical of eighteenth-century Polish
society as it "ought to be." Significantly, Krasicki's characters do
not have individual names, but are spoken of and addressed by
their rank or social status: so the narrator meets the Squire, the
Priest, the Chamberlain, the Colonel and the Colonel's Wife, just
as many characters in *Pan Tadeusz* are referred to throughout the
poem simply as the Count, the Usher, the Judge or the Steward. In
both novel and poem the characters are occupied for most of the
time in ordinary, everyday, even prosaic occupations—eating and
drinking, taking walks, visiting, and celebrating private occasions
such as birthdays or wedding feasts.

The Squire is a prototype of Mickiewicz's Judge Soplica, both
being concerned (and very properly, according to their authors)
with the importance of rank, precedence and order: so the narrator admires the "orderliness" of the Squire's estate (I, i, 8), the
Squire expatiates on the rules of hospitality (II, ii, 1), an activity
in which both host and guest have their ordained roles to play,

and there is even a squabble over precedence, though this does not take place at the Squire's house (II, ii, 7). The same preoccupation occurs on the Judge's estate at Soplicowo: every individual in this society has his or her right place in the scheme of things, and each moves within a precisely definable network of social relationships. The Squire frequently looks back with approval to manners and customs of the past, just as the Judge retains bygone traditions and ritual.

The Squire's local Priest appears frequently in Krasicki's work, as does Father Robak in *Pan Tadeusz:* Krasicki's comic Castellan, with his suite of "jockeys" and eccentric attire (III, iii, 1) foreshadows Mickiewicz's Count, who is also accompanied by "jockeys" and described by his author as "a great eccentric." Even the Squire's account of the way in which Polish gentry divide up country estates among the family heirs until, "in time, each village is crammed with heirs, gentry only by name, peasants in reality" (III, ii, 6) brings to mind the Dobrzynski clan, "forced to work for themselves,/ Like hired serfs" although they still pride themselves on their gentility (VI).

II *Characters*

Krasicki's characters in *The Squire* cannot be said to share the vitality and humanity of the protagonists of *Pan Tadeusz,* because their function is entirely different. Like the characters in *Nicholas Find-Out* they are little more than pretexts, introduced so that the Squire and his author can expatiate at length on a wide range of topics, on most of which (as we shall see) Krasicki had already expressed his opinions in the *Monitor,* the *Satires, Nicholas* and elsewhere.

Krasicki's characters look back to the "character sketches" of the seventeenth century, as practiced by La Bruyère and others. They are not to be regarded as individuals but as human types (Krasicki's habit of referring to his characters exclusively by their titles of rank or social appurtenance was mentioned above). As a rule they are briefly described on their first appearance: the narrator's meeting with the Squire when the book starts is characteristic of Krasicki's method, as we are informed that the Squire was "dressed in a white jacket, with a leather belt and wide straw-hat," and has a "serious countenance, ruddy complexion and grey mustache." When the Judge appears, he is described as "elderly, tall, bald, dry," wearing a "four-cornered cap, long robe and quilted jacket," while he and his wife "represent a picture of our grand-parents." (I, ii, 4). The Chamberlain is "a man of middle age, medium in stature, stout, with an agreeable countenance, and it was apparent that in his youth he had been boisterous and robust" (II, ii, 10).

Occasionally Krasicki offers a somewhat more detailed character sketch, as when the Squire gives an account of a fashionable lady not unlike the one described in Satire VIII. After a prolonged stay abroad, this lady decides to visit her country estate, which is close to that of the Squire. Two months before she arrives, a "French *tapissier*" appears with orders to "somehow transform the earlier barbarity of her manor-house." When the lady visits the Squire and his wife, they barely recognize her: she has "changed her manner of speaking, walking and dressing," and "seemed no longer the lady we had known." She opens the conversation by pitying "country-folk, who—to be sure—lead an innocent life, though this uniform innocence was, in her opinion, so boring that it would be better to be less innocent, and to amuse oneself more." Needless to say, Paris is her ideal, and the rest of the world nothing but "steppe, desert, wildness and barbarity."

Next day is Sunday, and the Squire sends to inform the lady that "Mass in our parish church begins at ten o'clock." He is alarmed when the servant returns to report the lady has "a migraine," and cannot attend the service. But on visiting her after Mass, the Squire and his wife find the lady in her boudoir "completely well and very merry." They congratulate her on this rapid recovery, and the Squire, noticing she has been reading a book, hopes it is a prayerbook. The lady thereupon retorts: "Ah! What a pity that you, sir, don't know French! What an inestimable writer is this Rajnal! How he inveighs against superstition, and attacks priests! How agreeable it is to read! and in addition, everyone can learn commerce from him, and discover how pepper, cinnamon and nutmeg reach us: how the Spaniards waged war, and killed Negroes . . ." The lady's author is the celebrated abbé Raynal, a "free-thinker" and "philosophe," associated with Diderot, Holbach and Grimm. His book, in which the "association of superstition and nutmeg" seemed strange to the Squire, was the widely read *History of Trade in the Indies* (1770) that went into thirteen editions in twenty years, and was published in a Polish translation in

1783. The last touch to the portrait comes when the Squire learns that, "bored with a week's stay in the country," the lady has departed for Town (II, iii, 4).

Though entertaining, the lady's portrait is not intended merely to entertain (we should remember that one of Krasicki's cardinal principles in writing was "to amuse while teaching"). The Squire's account of her behavior is introduced to give the Squire the opportunity to comment disapprovingly on her ways, and to contrast them, by implication, with the way ladies *should* behave.

Other character sketches are brief: when the Judge and his sons visit the Squire, we learn that the eldest (the Regent) reads too many romances; the second (the Lieutenant) passes his time in ladies' boudoirs; and the third (the Comrade in Arms) is a drunkard and brawler. The Squire, naturally, has a good deal to say on all these blameworthy vices. (I, ii, 4).

The settings in which we see the Squire and the other characters are also "representative" of eighteenth-century Poland. The Squire's manor-house has a "spacious yard" containing willow-trees and "four linden trees in the middle, a turf seat under each." To the right is a "well-ordered kitchen block, with rooms (as I remarked) for the servants." To the left are "stables, coach-houses, a brick granary with iron bars and shutters." The manor itself is "made of wood, on a good and well-elevated sub-structure of brick." The interior is described in the same brief terms (I, i, 1). The Squire and the narrator spend a considerable part of their time in the Squire's garden, which contains a "bower," and in Part I appears to be designed in the formal style contemptuously referred to by the "fashionable wife" as "German style." As the work proceeds, however, the Squire and his wife alter its style: in Part III, the garden contains a "Chinese bower" where the Squire's wife cultivates silk-worms, and "irregular thickets" as in English gardens have made their appearance.

On his way to and from the Squire's estate, the narrator has occasion to pass through villages and townships which provide a sharp contrast to the well-kept villages on the Squire's estate. When his carriage breaks down in one such, "the cottages were in the most miserable state, the people wretchedly dressed, and the children, almost naked, were rolling in the mud." On another occasion, the narrator remarks on the "greed of heirs and owners" of country estates, which makes Polish villages "abject and deserted, their dwellings like shacks rather than homes, the peasantry wretched, their children dying out for the most part from poverty and hunger." (II, ii, 12).

III *Themes*

The wretched state of the Polish peasantry at this time is one of the topics to which Krasicki reverts time and again. As we know, he was an author who never minded saying the same thing twice (or more often), providing he thought it true and useful. But by present-day standards, his attitude to serfdom is ambiguous: genuinely concerned with the miserable lot of the Polish peasantry—as were many of his enlightened contemporaries—Krasicki never recommended that serfdom be abolished in Poland. The institution was, to his mind, part of the natural order of things, though it was the moral duty of the gentry to improve the lot of their serfs. The Squire sets a good example in this respect: he has provided his serfs with houses to replace the "shacks in which our serfs usually dwell," he has established a village school in which peasant children learn to read, write, and count, and study the Catechism—an education suited to their station in life (I, ii, 2). There is a practical side to the Squire's benevolence: as he says "Not only humanity, but our own profit ought to cause us to treat our serfs well" (I, ii, 1).

Almost anything provides the Squire with material for a "discourse," and the conversation ranges from the benefits or harm of dancing, card-playing, hypochondria, litigation and the law-courts, and the latest fashions. A bottle of mead on the Squire's table gives him the cue for a long digression on drinking habits in Poland: his name and address on an envelope provide him with a pretext for satirizing the Poles' fondness for using obsolete titles. Some topics appear more often than others: education, both domestic and public, occupies much of the Squire's attention, so do hospitality, agriculture, gardening and travel.

Two topics which the Squire and his friends touch on but rarely are religion and politics. Apart from insisting on the importance of a pious, God-fearing upbringing for children, and the observance of such rites as attending Mass at the parish church, saying Grace at table and fasting at the proper time, the Squire does not concern himself with the mysteries of Christian faith. Krasicki's portrait of the Squire's piety is convincing, even down to the latter's

reminder that it is the gentry's duty to attend Mass as an example
to the lower orders.

The Squire's reluctance to talk about politics is explained in
part by Krasicki's own lack of interest in such matters (as witness,
for example, his private correspondence, in which political affairs
are rarely, if ever, mentioned—and Krasicki's correspondence
covers the last half of the eighteenth century that saw, for instance, the French Revolution). Partly, too, the events in Poland
of 1772—which, incidentally, made Krasicki himself a subject of
Frederick of Prussia—might be held responsible. Not that the
Squire refrains entirely from commenting on Poland's fate: in Part
I, for instance, he reminds the narrator " 'Love of homeland was
our fathers' motto; had they known . . .' tears came into his eyes,
and he ceased" (I, i, 6). Later, the Squire blames "our total ruin"
and "decline of the State" on the "nefarious children of virtuous
citizens" (I, ii, 5).

Apart from the digressions and moralizing, *The Squire* contains
much information on manners and customs in eighteen-century
Poland. We learn, for example, that Polish gentry, when travelling
to visit relatives or friends, usually took their own beds with them;
that visitors might be welcomed by the host firing a cannon in
their honor; that girls married young, and could be mothers at the
age of fourteen; that Polish roads were, for the most part, in a bad
state of repair, and that it was not uncommon for carriage wheels
to break, whereupon travelers were forced to seek refuge in
squalid inns. The narrator describes entering one such village tavern:

"the door was so low, that I had to stoop to half my height, and even
so I bruised my forehead. There was no floor, and geese were sitting
around the door in a puddle; coops full of hens surrounded a clay
stove, behind which newborn calves had a little stable. The room had
two windows, one half-covered with shingles, the other stopped up
with straw . . ." (II, i, 1).

To be sure, Krasicki was not concerned with providing his readers with information of this kind: primarily they, after all, regarded *The Squire*, with its type-characters and settings, as an
almost inexhaustible fount of moralizing. Today, moralizing is an
acquired taste, and it must be admitted that in any case Krasicki's
is not of a very high order. Though well-meant, it is moralizing

that comes less from the heart than from decorum and good manners. The Squire's morality derives from respectability, which deplores excess and has no place for the passions, for conflict, hope, frustration or despair. No one, at the present time, would describe *The Squire* (as Dmochowski, Krasicki's first editor, did) as "the most beautiful and useful work in any language." Nevertheless, for all the change in literary taste since that time, it is difficult to imagine the Polish Age of Enlightenment without Krasicki's *Squire*.

IV *History*

Although "modern" historiography dates from the eighteenth century (Gibbon, Naruszewicz, Voltaire and others), that age was curiously anti-historical. Enlightened people regarded with skepticism the writings of Roman historians, while in Poland, the ancient chronicles, with their accounts of legendary kings and mythical happenings, were no longer implicitly believed. Even the hitherto unchallenged certainties of Biblical history were dissolving under the scrutiny of chronologists who discovered inconsistencies and even contradictions in Holy Writ. The further back in time historical writings went, the less reliable they became: ancient history was so riddled with uncertainties that Voltaire believed the study of it merely a waste of sensible people's time. As he asserted: "History consists of a series of accumulated imaginative inventions."

Historical characters were challenged too. Persons like Alexander the Great or Attila the Hun were stripped of their heroic qualities and condemned as tyrants or enemies of mankind—the idea of despotism aroused strong feelings in the eighteenth century (and still stronger ones in the nineteenth). So Alexander the Great, hero of a popular "tale" which had many editions in sixteenth- and seventeenth-century Poland, was dethroned by enlightened persons, and his place taken instead by idealized figures of "virtue," such as Marcus Aurelius.

The first modern history of Poland was the work of Krasicki's contemporary, Adam Naruszewicz. Like Voltaire and Gibbon in Western Europe and Karamzin in Russia, Naruszewicz sought to bring the light of reason to bear on what hitherto been darkness, and to draw the line between history and legend.

Krasicki had already derided the legends and myths recorded in

the Polish chronicles by populating King Popieł's kingdom on
Lake Gopło with talking cats and mice (*Battle of Mice*). He returned to the attack on the "frivolity and impudence of chroni-
clers" [11] in his *History Divided into Two Books* (1779–1780). But
Krasicki's *History* is not wholly serious, and indeed comes close to
science fiction with a moral. Although the book was translated
into German in 1785, and into French in 1817, it was not reprinted
in Poland during Krasicki's lifetime. This suggests that the reading
public, who had eagerly bought copies of his *Fables*, the *Satires*,
the *Adventures of Nicholas Find-Out* and *The Squire* found the
History less interesting. They were "unable to decipher the metaphor" around which Krasicki structured the work. [12]

After a traditional flourish, in which Krasicki declares that the
manuscript of *History* was found in a roadside tavern in Poland,
he proceeds by means of a quotation from Swift's *Gulliver's Travels* III to express his indebtedness to that work: "According to the
celebrated Gulliver, an author of unquestionable reliability," certain individuals among the race known as the Strulbruggs are immortal, and "condemned without any Fault of their own, to a per-
petual Continuance in the World." Krasicki's narrator and author
of the manuscript, named Grumdrigg, is himself a member of this
unfortunate race. He too is immortal, and the *History* is his account of selected characters and incidents in world history from
the third century B.C. to medieval Poland.

By his nature, Grumdrigg is a suitable narrator for Krasicki's
satirical purpose in the *History*. Although he visits Greece, Rome,
Carthage, Spain, China and other places at various periods in
time, his immortality renders him a foreigner and "outsider"
everywhere, and he is completely non-partisan towards the historical figures and events he meets and witnesses. Consequently the
veracity of his narrative cannot be open to doubt, while he himself is the personification of enlightened sense, and measures
everything by reason.

One of the first historical characters Grumdrigg encounters on
his wanderings is none other than Alexander the Great, and in
view of the contempt in which Alexander was held by enlightened
minds in the eighteenth century, we may expect Grumdrigg's account of him to be colored with similar disapproval. Grumdrigg
describes him as "scheming for universal monarchy," "bold and
proud," and the description of his death follows very closely that

given by Swift in *Gulliver* III, where Gulliver is enabled to converse with Alexander's ghost. The ghost thereupon "assured me upon his Honour he was not poisoned, but dyed of a Fever by excessive Drinking." In *History,* Alexander is carried away intoxicated from a banquet to his bed, recommences his debauch next day, is again carried off to bed, develops a malignant fever and does not rise again (I, 3).

In contrast to Alexander, whose "actions made him more suited to a madhouse than the throne of the entire world" (I, 5), Krasicki proceeds to set up the figure of Ptolomy, a leader in Alexander's army and Grumdrigg's master. He is one of the many mild and charitable individuals in the book encountered by Grumdrigg, and they are, of course, objects of his approval and admiration.

After a sojourn in Egypt with Ptolomy, Grumdrigg proceeds to Carthage, where he stays during the Punic wars, waged by Rome against that city. Grumdrigg sees Carthage as an enlightened state, ruled by the idealized Hamilcar and Hannibal, model rulers all famous men would do well to emulate. Hamilcar, in particular, is deserving of Grumdrigg's approval: he is a patron of the sciences, his favorite reading consists of "useful works," he has "learned to control his passions for the benefit of his country," and is a benevolent landlord into the bargain.

In addition to hatred for such tyrants as Alexander the Great, Grumdrigg betrays a particular detestation for various other classical figures of authority, from Aristotle and Diogenes to Cicero, Livy, Plutarch and Seneca. Here Krasicki was making his contribution to the revolt against classical authorities that was taking place all over Europe. Voltaire set the fashion by attacking Diogenes (in the barrel), and in 1785 an English writer declared of Aristotle that "his work on poetry is a crude and undigested performance, written by the author in his silly vanity of dictating in every science then known by man." When Grumdrigg meets Aristotle, his comment is that the philosopher "knew more about court life than about philosophy," and he relished the "good wages" paid him as Alexander's tutor ("The philosophers of that age, too, were beginning not to despise wealth" (I, 4)). To an enlightened eighteenth-century mind, Aristotle and his authoritative poetic theory was inextricably associated with the pedantic excesses of scholasticism as practiced in the Jesuit schools.

Grumdrigg's account of a meeting with Cicero is equally deflat-
ing: the celebrated orator of classical antiquity reveals himself to
be highly susceptible to "the sweet incense of praise," while on
becoming Consul and saving Rome from Cataline's conspiracy, he
proves to be "intolerably loquacious" (I, 19). Seneca is depicted
by Grumdrigg as an usurer, and he accuses the Roman historian
Livy of "inconsistencies, inventions and purely rhetorical effects."
Livy, like other historians, is charged with being more of a "writer
of panegyrics than a historian of his homeland" (I, 8).

Although Grumdrigg's adventures span a period that covers the
emergence of Christianity, this topic is not mentioned. The eighteenth century was, as we have seen, a period when the certainties
of Biblical history were beginning to collapse. But a brief incident, in which Grumdrigg encounters Apollonius of Tiana (who
visits Imperial Rome under Augustus, while Grumdrigg is in the
city), and scoffs at the alleged "miracles" of the saint, may well be
based on a notorious lampoon of the New Testament by the Deist
Charles Blount, published in London in 1680.[13] This little work
was the forerunner of the rejection by enlightened persons of
parts of the New Testament that were not (they thought) recon-
cilable with common sense and rational knowledge. That Krasicki
was familiar with Blount's lampoon is suggested by the fact that a
French translation was made in 1774 at the instigation of the free-
thinking Frederick II of Prussia (with a second edition in 1779).
Krasicki spent most winters after 1772 at Frederick's court and
cannot have avoided obtaining a first-hand knowledge of deistic
doctrines, fashionable not only at Frederick's court, but also at
all the "enlightened" courts of Europe, and among the higher
ranks of the clergy. Deism was, essentially, a belief in the existence
of a Supreme Being, accompanied by a rejection of the mystic
elements that Christianity had accrued.

In one respect, Krasicki's *History* foreshadows a characteristically Polish development of the novel, that was to occur throughout the nineteenth century, when writers used fiction as a mask
for expressing their own ideas on contemporary matters that could
not—because of the censorship or other reasons—be openly discussed. Historical novels were particularly suited to this kind of
treatment, and readers quickly became adept at divining hidden
meanings: for instance, *Quo Vadis?* by Henryk Sienkiewicz
(1895) was "interpreted" (whether rightly or wrongly) as depict-

ing the struggle of the recently-formed Socialist movement (represented by the early Christians) against a tyrannical Tsar (the Emperor Nero in the novel).

Thus, when Grumdrigg visits ancient Gaul, tyrannically oppressed by the Romans under the "barbarian" Julius Caesar, who "founded his own glory on injustice to others, perpetrating a genuine evil for superficial good" (II, 4), he encounters the Druid High Priest Astiorynx, who enquires: "What benefit have the Romans' unjust victories brought them? Believe me, the edifice, shoddily put together, will destroy itself by its own magnitude and, weakened by its own weight, will collapse" (*ibid.*). The example of Poland, subjugated by the enormous and ever-expanding power of the Russian empire at once comes to mind. Krasicki is writing in the prophetic vein of his "Romantic" successors, and expects his readers to perceive the allusions.

As already noticed, the *History* is cast in the form of a "manuscript accidentally found" and published in an incomplete form by its editor. The fragmentary state of the work (Book II ends in the middle of a sentence, while Book III consists only of chapters V to X, again breaking off with the editor's laconic remark "There is no more") relates it to Lawrence Sterne's *Tristram Shandy* and *Sentimental Journey*, with their lack of conventional endings and deliberate disorder. Both were read and admired in eighteenth-century Poland, though their literary influence did not have full effect until the next generation. But Krasicki's deliberate use of the fragmentary as a form of literary composition in its own right demonstrates how closely he followed and understood the trends of contemporary European literature. His version of MacPherson's fraudulent *Ossian* (London 1765, Warsaw 1790) will provide further evidence of Krasicki's catholic attitude towards modern European writing.

V "Entertaining Trifles"

Krasicki continued his self-imposed task of familiarizing Polish readers with what was most instructive, interesting and entertaining in contemporary European literature by composing a number of "oriental tales"—a genre that flourished during the Age of Enlightenment.[14] These tales derived from the publication of the collection known as *The Arabian Nights*, translated by Antoine Galland (Paris, 1704–1717), a work so different in character from anything then known, that its impact on European literature can only be compared to the re-discovery of Roman and Greek classical literature in the fifteenth century.

To be sure, Galland dressed up his version of the Turkish original in eighteenth-century costume, and omitted the coarse, sometimes pornographic tales that were not made accessible to Western readers until Richard Burton's version appeared late in the nineteenth century. Even so, the tales were too fantastic to be imitated by the writers of the Age of Enlightenment. However, it was not long before these writers perceived that tales populated by exotic sultans, wise men, dervishes and Brahmins, and located in distant, almost totally unknown places like Aleppo, Bagdad, Damascus, Cairo or the Taurus could be profitably used for more serious purposes than mere entertainment. Like the improbable talking animals and objects of fables and mock-heroic poems, oriental tales made a useful vehicle for satire, philosophy or pointing a moral. In France, the philosophical satirist Montesquieu found such tales a suitable means for oblique criticism of his own society (*Lettres persanes,* 1721), and Voltaire utilized the genre in *Zadig* (1748) to express his philosophical notions and to satirize contemporary society. Oriental tales also have their place in English literature of the eighteenth century, where they were practiced by writers from Addison to Dr. Johnson and William Beckford.

Krasicki naturally became familiar with many of these examples of the oriental tale, and his own include versions of tales by Montesquieu, Goldsmith and Dr. Johnson (*Seged,* which he translated from a French version without acknowledging the English original). Several of Krasicki's tales are of the philosophical kind, designed by their author to illustrate such themes as the vanity of human wishes, the transitory nature of human life, the inevitability of death, or the pursuit of happiness, fame and riches defeating its own ends. So, despite all his endeavors, Krasicki's Seged, the ruler of Ethiopia, is forced by a series of experiences to state that "No man should ever presume to say, 'This day shall be a day of happiness.'" *The Deacon of Badajoz,* although set in Spain, is nonetheless identical in spirit and style with the oriental tales: in it, Krasicki dwells on the vanity of earthly things, as the Deacon rises to Bishop, Archbishop and finally Cardinal—only to be reduced to his first humble rank in the course of a few moments. The *Deacon* also illustrates human ingratitude, demon-

strated in *Rustan,* where wild animals (a lion, snake and mon-
key) display more gratitude than mankind.

Other tales point a moral, *i.e.* they take the side of virtue and
common sense, seek to show how a man should live, and demonstrate that love, friendship, and virtuous, altruistic conduct are the
best and probably the only ways of achieving happiness in this
world. The tale *Ibrahim and Osman* illustrates this: walking by
the Nile in Cairo, Osman boasts that he strictly observes Ramadan, frequents the mosques, and has visited Mecca and the
Prophet's tomb in Medina. Ibrahim admits "with a sigh" that he
was unable to make the pilgrimage to Mecca, on account of a
circumstance which prevented him from experiencing that happiness—"one of the greatest a true believer can have in this life."
Osman inquires what the circumstance was, but Ibrahim declines
to answer. Later, Ibrahim is visited in a dream by a "solemn personage," who informs him that while it is a great service to visit
the grave of the Prophet, yet Ibrahim's remaining at the sick-bed
of his uncle Hassan was still greater. Osman's pilgrimage has been
weighed in heavenly scales, and found wanting: Ibrahim's absence weighed twice as heavily, and now weighs ten times more,
since "through modesty, you did not say why you were absent."

The folly of being dissatisfied with the station allotted one in
life is illustrated by the tale *Hamid:* after reading the idyllic and
pastoral poems of Sa'di, Hamid, son of a rich merchant in Aleppo,
decides to lead an idyllic and pastoral life himself, only to discover that the reality of a shepherd's life in the mountains of Leb-
anon is very different from the life pictured by the poet: inspired
by a book on modern theories of agriculture, Hamid acquires a
farm and cultivates modern methods, only to go bankrupt: a book
dealing with the feats of famous men makes Hamid join the army
in search of glory, but he is wounded and left for dead on the
battle-field. Other disillusioning experiences follow, until the unfortunate Hamid has learned his lesson.

In addition to looking back to the characteristic eighteenth-
century fondness for moralizing and philosophizing in fiction,
Krasicki's oriental tales also look forward to Romanticism. In particular, his use of exotic words like "pasha," "Koran," "Allah,"
"ramadan," "mosque," personal names such as "Ibrahim,"
"Osman," "Rustan," and place-names like Aleppo, Bagdad, the
Nile and the Ganges foreshadow the *Crimean Sonnets* of Adam

Mickiewicz (1826), where Turkish and Persian words play a part in Mickiewicz's revolt against eighteenth-century poetic diction, and which his "classical" contemporaries found barbarous. Their appearance demonstrates yet again that Krasicki, in his distant retreat at Heilsberg, continued to be fully aware of the contemporary literary situation in Western Europe.

CHAPTER 8

The Epistolary Art

ALTHOUGH Krasicki kept up a voluminous correspondence all his life (see Chapter 11), he also practiced a different kind of letter-writing, and in 1780 he published a set of *Epistles*, or verse letters. Yet again, Horace provides the classical model for this genre.

Krasicki referred to his epistles as a "kind of satire," and they are close to satires in both spirit and structure. To be sure, they are all addressed to various individuals whom Krasicki knew, and in this sense can be regarded as personal communications. But the "center of gravity" in a verse epistle (and those of Krasicki are no exception) is not so much in a communication between individuals, as in the ideas expounded. Horace's Epistle to Numicius ("Nil admirari," I, 6), for instance, is a miniature treatise on practical philosophy, in which Horace condemns ambition and cupidity.[1] His "Ars poetica" (II, 3) is, similarly, a treatise on literary theory. Krasicki's epistles treat of a number of topics of immediate relevance to his contemporaries—from the art of politics, to social life and moral or ethical speculations.

At first sight, these topics may seem little suited to be rendered in poetry. But we may suppose Krasicki's reasoning followed that of Alexander Pope, who declared in the preface to his own four epistles known as *The Essay on Man* (1734–35):

I chose verse, and even rhyme, for two reasons. The one will appear obvious; that principles, maxims or precepts so written, both strike the reader more strongly at first, and are more easily retained by him afterwards. The other may seem odd, but is true. I found I could express them more shortly this way than in prose itself; and nothing is more certain, than that much of the force as well as grace of arguments or instructions, depends on their conciseness.

I *Epistles I–IV*

The structure of Krasicki's epistles follows the classical pattern, in which all the parts are intended to persuade the person addressed (and the reader) to accept the writer's arguments. The first epistle, addressed to King Stanislas Augustus, begins with an *exordium,* in which Krasicki addresses him directly: "Is it right to inquire, your majesty?/ People say, and many are of the opinion,/ That kings have never had friends . . ." Now follows the *narratio,* in which Krasicki announces his topic: is this statement—that kings were always friendless—still true? Krasicki professes he is reluctant to believe so, and the third stage of the epistle (*probatio*) contains the bulk of the writer's arguments, as he sets out his terms and advances proofs. A king without friends would deserve pity, rather than envy: a throne is an eminent position to occupy, but "what's its use, when no one loves its occupant?" Man, after all, is a social animal.

Krasicki now passes to his *refutatio,* in which the writer puts forward objections his addressee may raise against the arguments put forward in the preceding section, and answers them himself: he refuses, for example, to believe Voltaire's "witty line" in which he called monarchs "worthy ingrates," nor (Krasicki protests) is he flattering the king—"I despise that craft."

Finally, Krasicki sums up his arguments in the *peroratio,* where, after stating some acceptable truths in the form of maxims ("Fate elevates . . . but he who is master of his fate, knows how to give and take . . ."), he offers the king his last piece of advice in a neatly-turned couplet: "Like an ingenious gardener who knows where to graft or to cut/ You will prove Voltaire a liar amidst your friends."

Epistle II (1782) is addressed to Christopher Szembek, a Church dignitary, and in it Krasicki expatiates on a topic he announces in the first line: "Fanaticism . . ." His main target in the epistle is the "common herd" of conservative and benighted gentry whom Krasicki and his enlightened contemporaries (including Szembek, an active member of the Senate on the side of social and educational reforms) had for two decades been trying to bring to reason.

The oratorical tone of Epistle II (indeed, all Krasicki's epistles are strongly oratorical) is heightened by the introduction of a number of personifications, intended to help define more closely what Krasicki means by "Fanaticism." The vice is neither "cruelty" nor "uncouthness," and there are many varieties of it, for it is "changeable and treacherous,/ Worst when it is the all-powerful mistress of Reason." It possesses "numerous armies," can slyly occupy entire neighborhoods and "like a conflagration, wherever it spreads its power,/ Everywhere destroys, lays waste, devours and consumes."

Fanaticism can also be recognized by its companion vice Barbarism and by a train of followers including Envy, Revenge, Blindness and Stupidity, all of which "terrify us by their impudence, and conquer by importunity."

Having established his topic, Krasicki proceeds to relate these personifications to contemporary life, which he sees threatened by Fanaticism and the other vices. For Fanaticism "rules by blind instinct, not by reason," and consequently from it spring "manifold errors which have destroyed entire States," not to mention the "notorious cry: Let things be as they always were!" and the rejection of "sound counsel" on the grounds that it is "novel." Here, Krasicki is offering a comment on the manner in which a majority of the gentry had rejected reforms proposed by Szembek in the Polish Parliament that same year—an incident that prompted Krasicki to inscribe the epistle.

What, then, must be done? Krasicki has no doubt as to the remedy: "We must fight against the common herd," for "Error can kindle ever-new prejudices,/ Can sanctify guilt, give immorality a gloss,/ And counter salutary work." As ever, Krasicki is able to provide relevant classical allusions to support his arguments and illuminate his meaning. He recalls Lycurgus, the half-legendary creator of the State of Sparta "happy for granting his homeland laws" though he lost an eye. Then again (Krasicki rhetorically inquires) what benefit had Socrates from condemning the crimes of Athenians? After all, "the common herd held him up to ridicule on the public stages,/ And finally he took the reward for his services by losing his life."

As in the *Epistles* of Horace, the general content that has hitherto dominated over personal interest, yields place in the concluding lines to particular advice addressed to Szembek. He is told that though it may be sweet to die for one's country, genuine heroism consists rather in being innocent though judged guilty, and in serving that country even in the face of ingratitude and slander.

Krasicki's first two epistles were addressed to eminent persons in contemporary life. In the third epistle, however, he addresses an almost anonymous "Paul," who has since been identified.[2] We shall respect Krasicki's preference here, because he was doubtless following closely on Horace—whose epistles were also addressed variously to eminent persons known to all Roman society, as well as to personal acquaintances of the poet, into whose identity we need not inquire.

Krasicki, like his classical model, announces his epistolary topic in the first line: "Where there is no obligation, is it good to trust?" then proceeds for the remainder of the poem to develop, examine and argue the notion in oratorical fashion. He examines criteria for judging and evaluating Man, and confides in Paul that he has chosen to indite this epistle to him, rather than to anyone else because Paul "knows how to humor the human species," so that Krasicki's confidences will not harm him.

Among these confidences made to Paul, Krasicki expresses one of the literary principles to which he held steadfastly throughout his career as a writer: "Many men paint portraits; the results vary;/ Some paint too black, others lay on too much white;/ But I am one of those, my dear Paul, who render things diverting." No matter which literary genre he is practicing, the writer must never bore his readers: if he does, the moral lesson he wishes to impart will not be communicated.

Briefly stated, Krasicki's argument is that the "basic, primary science" in human life is that of "knowing Man." To achieve this knowledge, we must be well armed with Virtue, and bear in mind too, that "things are not what they seem." We ourselves are frequently to blame because we do not look at Man aright. The world after all, is a great theater, and men the actors—not an entirely new idea, to be sure, but appropriate in this context. Finally, he comes to the conclusion that prudence is man's best guide in life, though unless applied with moderation, even this virtue can lead to misanthropy.

A topic to which Krasicki had already turned his satirical attention on numerous occasions reappears in Epistle IV, addressed to Prince Stanislas Poniatowski, the king's nephew: this is the mania for extravagant "Grand Tours" by wealthy aristocrats and gentry.

Krasicki's view on the topic is announced immediately: "First of all, Your Highness, you must know,/ That if it is good to travel, it is still better to stay home." After elaborating on this maxim, Krasicki inquires why the Prince has decided to travel—and, as often, supplies his own answer: "Fashion decrees" that members of polite society should travel for their health to drink the waters at Carlsbad or Spa, though if this remedy does not cure the "spasms and vapors," the sufferer must have recourse to doctors. They, in turn, can only be found in Paris, the "capital of tender feelings." For such a trip, however, entire villages in Poland must be sold to meet expenses, and when the victim (usually a woman) returns to her homeland (as did the widow Krasicki satirized in *The Squire*), she "has forgotten how to speak Polish, nor does she know what grits are,/ Monotonous Polish dances enervate her nerves,/ Polish costume and whiskers make her swoon," and nothing can compare in her eyes to Versailles and the Louvre.

In the next section, Krasicki derides the extravagance of great landowners when they visit their country estates, accompanied by a "numerous court" of hangers-on and toadies, ranging from a personal physician to a pastrycook, not to mention a "Swiss philosopher, a gloomy Englishman, and a talkative Frenchman" to add tone and elegance to the visit. To be sure, Krasicki is exaggerating for satiric effect, but contemporary memoirs, journals and letters provide ample evidence that the nobility of the eighteenth century squandered enormous fortunes on luxury in much the same way as the aristocracy of Imperial Rome had done: nor was this extravagance confined to Poland.

Not until the final paragraph of his epistle does Krasicki hasten to assure the prince that the satire does not apply to him: "So act others—not you!" Nevertheless, Krasicki evidently feels it his moral duty to warn the prince against the courtiers surrounding him—a species for whom Krasicki always had a strong antipathy.

I   *Epistles V–VIII*

Krasicki continues his exploration of the ever-interesting topic of patriotism in Epistle V, addressed to his brother Antoni, and entitled "On a Citizen's Duties." By dwelling on the affectionate relationship subsisting between his brother and himself, Krasicki is able to make a neat transition by declaring "We are children of the same mother—but our mother is in misfortune." The point he is making here is clarified by the couplet in which he reminds his brother that "the greatest honor is to be a citizen among free men./I *was* one, you still are . . ." His brother, living in Eastern Poland, had not yet been affected by the partitions, the first of which (1772) made Krasicki—as the Bishop of Warmia—a subject of Frederick of Prussia.

After praising the "simplicity and antique virtue" of their forebears, Krasicki restates the eighteenth-century belief that "In every place, and at every time, Man is always Man,/The same tendencies are in us, as they were in men centuries ago." Man needs to be happy, but Krasicki warns his reader that excessive freedom may well be a source of misfortune, while "he who wishes to err—yet go unpunished" will never be accounted a patriot. Krasicki is once again stating his case against the reactionary, quarrelsome Polish gentry of the time, and he supports that case by a reminder that the civil wars of ancient Greece brought about the country's fall. He concludes the epistle with an exhortation to his fellow-countrymen to "respect their own privileges," lest they lose them.

In 1780, Adam Naruszewicz began publishing his monumental *History of the Polish Nation,* and Krasicki, who was on good terms with his eminent contemporary, celebrated the occasion by composing the epistle that forms number VI in the collection. Naturally enough, Krasicki takes the opportunity to restate—this time in verse—some of his own enlightened views on the writing and study of history, implied a year earlier in the *History.*

After remarking on the manner in which the passage of time reduces historical figures ("though eminent, celebrated, powerful and rich") until we finally see that each is "only a bad man, or a good one," Krasicki considers some of the main difficulties encountered in the writing of history: the historiographer must know how "to debase where necessary, and where to elevate,/To show how things work out in the world,/To maintain a golden mean between flattery and slander,/To draw the essence of things from its proper source . . ." The historiographer must not "conceal or invent" anything "for love of his own country," nor boast descent from heroes of classical antiquity—a boast sometimes made by ignorant Polish gentry.

But Naruszewicz (so Krasicki assures his reader) will dismiss all the "fairy-tales," legends and fictions that had accumulated in history, and in doing so, Naruszewicz will "guard the Truth," for Truth is the "essence of things." Without it, "charm of style" and "Art" are of no avail.

Krasicki returns yet again to the attack on certain historical figures already noticed in his own *History*, charging the "common herd" with admiring "Fame acquired by impiety and force:/ He is accounted great, who conquered and oppressed others,/He who conquered the weak by force,/ He who made thousands wretched . . ." Krasicki, more enlightened, knows that Truth sets a greater store on Virtue and Humanity than on Courage: he again holds up Alexander the Great as an example, and declares that Alexander deserves to be remembered, not for his military prowess and victories, but because he showed mercy to the womenfolk of his enemy Darius. In contrast to military leaders and tyrants, Krasicki presents King Casimir the Great, regarded in the Age of Enlightenment as a wise, peace-loving king, concerned with political reforms and controlling the power of the Polish nobles. But since the times of Casimir "our nation has grown weak, our neighbors more powerful," and Poland now "has become the spoils of others." In the final exhortation, Krasicki urges the historian to inform his readers of these unhappy matters, for to "admit the error" of their past ways is already a step towards Virtue, and "to despair is an abject thing."

The penultimate epistle (VII) is lighter in tone, as Krasicki examines (not without irony) the fate of creative writers including his own in eighteenth-century Poland. He addresses a certain Rotkiewicz, one of King Stanislas' secretaries, who had rendered Krasicki a service by copying manuscripts for him during a stay in Warsaw in 1780. He formulates certain literary principles for the edification of Rotkiewicz, beginning with the Horatian maxim: "Before we start to write, we must earnestly consider,/ Whether we are competent to end that which we are undertaking,/ But as conceit is often a prime consideration,/ We often err in the account." Consequently, many a would-be writer finds himself exposed to derision, and may indeed find it more profitable to write promissory notes—like "Mr. Bartholomew, who is not very learned, but a great writer of promissory notes," and who possesses an "easy style, certain profit, and celebrity without risk."

Krasicki urges Rotkiewicz to consider the lot of a writer such as "Blazej" (himself), who was "shouted down by Father Alphonse" (an allusion to the uproar caused by the publication of the *Battle of Monks*), "laughed at by Julia" (from *Nicholas Find-Out*), and "angered the Squire." Plaintively he asks "What's the use of post-humous fame, if writers starve when alive?" Only a few years earlier, Naruszewicz had complained in similar tones of the lot of writers in Augustan Poland. In a satire called "The Starveling Author" (1772), Naruszewicz describes an unfortunate literary hack who "hasn't a penny in his purse, and is up to his ears in debt" because (as the Starveling Author says) "The day has not yet dawned in our country/ When everyone reads useful books at home." Instead, they protest they "have no time for reading." Even his printer is accused of "skinning" the author. We know from his correspondence that Naruszewicz himself always found literature an "unprofitable business," and the starveling author's sarcastic remark about his printer is reminiscent of Naruszewicz's complaint that his own publisher, Gröll, was demanding 25 per cent of the profits on Naruszewicz's *History of the Polish Nation*. Other poets of the age who harped on the wretched lot of writers includued Franciszek Karpiński and Franciszek Zablocki (the author of "The Lay of a Poverty-Stricken Literary Man"). Krasicki is forced to the conclusion that literature in Poland is still dependent upon the patronage of the wealthy. The age that promised so much when King Stanislas Augustus came to the throne over a decade earlier had not fulfilled all its promise.

The cycle ends on a lighter, though still characteristic note, with a satirical lament to Antoni Lucinski, who holds the traditional office of the King's cupbearer. Krasicki sympathizes with Lucinski for this supposedly "low" appointment, concerned as it was with "flasks, barrels and drunkenness." However, he reminds his correspondent that the office of cupbearer was not always held in contempt. Harking back to the "good old days," the poet sings the praises of Poland's national drinks, mead and beer, even though they are despised "nowadays" since they can be had easily and cheaply, and the peasantry drink them. Yet, in the "old days," for all the consumption of these beverages, "sobriety was the honor of young and old," and with sobriety "courage, steadfastness, and hard work" brought Poland fame in foreign lands. In those days, too, the Poles were "awe-inspiring, wealthy and happy." Although Krasicki assures Lucinski that he does not condemn the drinking of expensive foreign wines by those who can afford to do so, he himself urges a return to wholesome national beverages, accompanied (needless to say) by moderation in their use.

The cycle of epistles, though not Krasicki's best-known or most popular work, demonstrates yet again his ability to handle almost any topic—from patriotic or moral duties and the art of writing, to the drinking of Polish beer—and to convert that topic into elegant and witty (if untranslatable) poetry that bears all the marks of his inimitable style.

CHAPTER 9

The Comedies

NO sooner had King Stanislas Augustus been elected to the throne in 1764, than he commanded the establishment of a National Theater in Warsaw. Hitherto, theaters in Poland had been either the private property of cultivated aristocrats, developed for their own entertainment, or school theaters organized by religious orders (especially the Jesuits), in which the sons of gentry took part in moralizing dramas for their own edification. The aristocratic theaters presented opera and ballet, often performed by French or Italian companies imported for the purpose. The ecclesiastical theaters, on the other hand, presented didactic plays, often performed in Latin.

Stanislas Augustus's aim in establishing Poland's National Theater was, essentially, to "amuse and educate" audiences. He regarded the theater in much the same light as his contemporary Catherine the Great of Russia, who also encouraged the establishment (in the same year) of the first permanent Russian theatrical company. Both these enlightened rulers saw the theater as yet another useful instrument for instilling higher standards of morality, virtue, manners and patriotic duty in the gentry who constituted the largest section of the audiences.

Krasicki shared the king's views on the function of the theater (although he did not write his comedies until the late 1770's). But articles Krasicki published in the *Monitor* for 1765 attest that he believed the theater was as important a secular institution as schools, books or moralizing journals and that it could, like satire, mock and condemn such faults in social morality as superstition, drunkenness, extravagance or the slavish imitation of foreign fashion, and, by appealing to the audience's reason, could even provide new and improved principles of rational conduct. He also believed that the stage could play its part in the purification of the Polish language.

By 1766, the National Theater had established a repertoire of plays by Polish writers, among whom the Jesuit Franciszek Bohomolec was the most prolific (at this time, Bohomolec was a co-editor with Krasicki of the *Monitor*). Bohomolec learned the craft of playwriting by adapting French or Italian originals for performance at ecclesiastical schools. To encourage other writers to produce plays for the National Theater, Krasicki turned his attention to the technique of playwriting, remarking in another *Monitor* essay that the rules for composing plays were not equally well-known to all. Audiences, too, were not always properly informed as to the "rules" by which they could evaluate the plays they saw or read.

In accordance with eighteenth-century critical theory (as laid down by Boileau and others), Krasicki points out that these "rules" were not "invented by writers," but were "drawn from Nature itself." He proceeds to discuss their application in the dramaturgy of classical antiquity and of Molière. The excellence of plays by these authors is largely due (so Krasicki suggests) to their strict observation of the "three unities" (place, time, action), which were supposed to add verisimilitude to plays, and the way in which the playwrights observed the requirements of decorum —elevated characters and language being reserved for tragedy, "low" characters and language being admissible to comedy. The two modes should never be mixed.

All Krasicki's views on playwriting are characteristically those of the widely-accepted literary theory of the Age of Enlightenment—although now this theory seems the height of artificiality and convention. It is all the more surprising, therefore, to find in the next issue of the *Monitor*, published only a few days later, a spirited attack on the "rules" for playwriting, by none other than Stanislas Augustus himself (which was the reason why Krasicki, as editor, had to publish it). The fact is that Stanislas Augustus was an admirer of the plays of Shakespeare, although to most thinking men of the Age of Reason, Shakespeare was a particularly "barbarous" writer. As a playwright, Shakespeare appeared to have gone out of his way to ignore the "rules"; he jumbled together "elevated" and "low" characters and styles in tragedy (the Porter in *Macbeth*); he took liberties with the unities (*A Winter's Tale*); his subjects were often "indecorous," and included murders and duels, not to mention the appearance of ghosts, witches and fairies. In a word, Shakespeare stood for many of the barbarian relics of the past which rational people like Krasicki were trying to abolish in Poland.

To be sure, Krasicki and other writers of the age had to admit that Shakespeare's plays occasionally contained "expressions worthy of the highest admiration and feeling; but he was unequal in inspiration, often overdoes his effects by excessive effort, and sometimes sinks so low that it is almost impossible to believe the plays were the work of the same author." In view of these faults, no rational author could think of taking the plays of Shakespeare as a model for his own.

Krasicki was well aware that the new National Theater in Warsaw was an innovation in Polish culture, and that writers of plays for its repertoire had few traditions in which to seek models. He therefore turned—like his contemporaries in Russia—to Molière, even though the French playwright had died nearly a century earlier. Despite this, the influence, prestige, and authority of Molière in the theater of Eastern Europe and Russia can hardly be overestimated. Poland and Russia were "Molière's second homeland," [1] though writers in Eastern Europe—for all their admiration and effort to imitate Molière—lacked his essential quality of genius.

They admired Molière for reasons different from those of present-day criticism. What mattered to them was Molière's skill in handling the all-important "unities." His *Misanthrope* was considered "perfect," mainly because its action takes the same time to perform on the stage as it would "in real life." His comedies also afforded Polish playwrights with the opportunity to moralize and satirize contemporary society. Polish playwrights (and Krasicki, when he came to compose his own) were hardly at all concerned with the reforms in playwrighting and stage-craft which Diderot and Beaumarchais were introducing into the theaters of Paris at this time. Nor were they interested in the dramaturgy of Marivaux, with his "études de métaphysique amoureuse," dealing with inner conflict and the analysis of feelings, expressed in refined language.

The plays of Molière most admired and imitated in Eastern Europe were his comedies of character, in which the writer's aim was to satirize a "universal" character personifying some human vice, fault or foible. The plot of a comedy of character was designed to expose or ridicule the character, while the play usually bore a title identifying the character and his or her vice (Molière's *Miser*, *Misanthrope* and *Imaginary Invalid*, for example).

Yet Molière's comedies of character had been an indirect cause for the decline in the genre on the French stage. His genius paralyzed two generations of French dramatists,[2] and comedy of character soon ceased attracting the best French playwrights. They realized they could not compete with their illustrious predecessor's exposés of human vice and folly, so turned instead to comedies in which plot and situation predominated. Molière almost exhausted the somewhat limited range of the major vices of human nature, and his imitators were reduced to deriding superficial foibles or eccentricities. Nevertheless the prestige of the comedy of character remained high throughout the eighteenth century, and the French stage continued to be populated by comedies satirizing characters who were irresolute, mischievous, absent-minded or self-important.

Krasicki's eight comedies include comedies of character that conform to the French model, though they also incorporate elements of other kinds of comedy too, particularly the comedy of manners. To begin with, their titles prepare the audience for the vice or folly to be satirized: *The Liar*, *The Fop*, *The Wiseacre*, and *The Litigant*. In these plays, everything focusses on the character who personifies the vice satirized. Minor characters may also be derided for various faults (drunkenness, credulity, affectation, imitation of foreign manners and costume, even novel-reading).

Another feature of the comedy of character are the "speaking names" Krasicki bestows on his characters. Just as English playwrights of the period crowded the London stage with characters improbably named "Mr. Novelty Fashion," "Sir Fopling Flutter," "Sir Tunbelly Clumsey," "Mr. Smirk" (a parson), "Lady Easy" and "Miss Mincing," so Krasicki introduces "Mr. Myslicki" ("Cogitator"), "Captain Tarabanski" ("Big Drum"), "Staruszkiewicz" ("Old Fellow"), "Wiatrakowski" ("Windmill"—a fashionable fop) and "Figlacki" ("Joker"—a servant). The purpose of the names was to make such characters instantly recognizable: as soon as the audience heard a "speaking name," they could at once identify the character's leading trait. Not all the characters bear a "speaking name," however: the heroes, heroines and "positive" characters bear conventional names, most of which are not even Polish—"Leander," "Leonora," "Erast," "Arist" and "Kunegunda" all appear. But these names, and others like them, are familiar from the French theater, and the fact that these people have no surnames need not surprise us.

Krasicki's settings are also familiar from eighteenth-century plays, which are said to take place in the house of the main character. No special decor or setting is required, partly because neither Krasicki's own theater nor the National Theater in Warsaw (where three of the plays were produced) were equipped for elaborate productions, and partly because the plays were intended to represent characters and settings the audience would recognize as "characteristic" of contemporary society.

One feature of eighteenth-century comedy lacking from Krasicki's plays are caricatures of real individuals, whom the audience could recognize. The introduction of such portraits was a powerful weapon in the hands of playwrights wishing to attack their rivals or enemies by ridiculing them on the stage. But Krasicki never indulged in personal malice or attacks on individuals, and indeed refers to the custom of writing lampoons as a " vile trade."

I *Characters*

As we should expect from the absurd "speaking names" and the colorless conventional names which Krasicki gives his characters, these personages are not intended to bear much resemblance to human beings. But Krasicki was not seeking to represent the complexities of real life. On the contrary, he had to reduce his characters and plots to the simplest possible terms, in order to concentrate all attention on the "ruling passion" by which the central characters are marked. So these persons—Anzelm the litigant, Obmowski the malicious satirist, the extravagant Leander and the others—are surrounded by a gallery of stereotypes ranging from a "raisonneur," through insipid heroes and heroines to the witty and ingenious valet and maid-servant. That Krasicki saw little or no necessity to individualize this gallery of stereotypes is indicated by the way in which he bestows the same name on characters in different plays: a "Leander" appears in both *The Celebrant* and *The Litigant,* a witty servant "Figlacki" (Joker) in *The Politician* and *The Litigant,* and "Staruszkiewicz" (Old Fellow) in *The Celebrant* and *The Satirist.*

The most important of the stereotypes is the "raisonneur," a rational and virtuous character who acts as spokesman for the author's views, though his role in the play's intrigue is often slight. Sometimes the raisonneur is the uncle of the character whose particular vice is being satirized, and he teaches his foolish nephew a lesson by threatening to disinherit him. Though taken in at first by the wit of his nephew "Obmowski" (Slanderer), Staruszkiewicz finally sees through his hypocrisy and malice, just in time to settle his fortune on another nephew. A "Staruszkiewicz" also appears in *The Celebrant,* to deplore Leander's extravagance and mania for surrounding himself with courtiers, secretaries and troops, as though he were a magnate. The raisonneur in *The Politician* is appropriately named "Roztropski" (Sensible) and in the first scene of the play he announces his intention of dissuading "Cogitator" from his various "foolish and strange plans." "Cogitator" himself is an example of an eighteenth-century Polish gentleman taken in by various charlatans who attempt to involve him in high-sounding but nonsensical commercial and agricultural projects, characteristic of this period as a result of the new "scientific" spirit abroad. Aryst, the brother of Anzelm (*The Litigant*), argues against this vice at some length, but in vain: the comedy ends with Anzelm about to embark on yet another law-suit, this time against his own daughter and her betrothed. As in the satire on drunkenness, with its last line in which the tables are turned on the moralizing narrator, so here Krasicki implies he is only too well aware that no amount of rational talk or satirical mockery is likely to cure a human vice or folly. The least he can do is to remind his audience and hope the lesson will not be lost on them.

The raisonneurs do not merely fulminate against vices and follies: they also expatiate on more "positive" themes, of which the most important are the obligations and duties of the gentry, which include the necessity of treating serfs in a humane manner.

Other stereotypes in the gallery Krasicki uses to populate his comedies are the hero and heroine, who do not resemble their present-day namesakes of drama. For the most part, they are passive and insipid creatures who express their feelings in high-flown language (which relates them to the heroes and heroines of sentimental comedy or "comèdie larmoyante"—a sub-species of the genre which became fashionable in Warsaw in the late 1770's). Were it not for the help of their servants (maid and valet respectively), in whom they confide, neither hero nor heroine would ever succeed in their courtships. This state of affairs, of course, prevailed on the French stage too. Indeed, witty and ingenious slaves had played important roles in the intrigues of classical Roman comedy (Plautus, Terence), and in the Italian *commedia dell'arte*.

Examples in Krasicki's comedies include Erast's valet "Figlacki" in *The Politician*, who disguises himself as "Doctor Pankracius" and tricks the "Cogitator" into bestowing his daughter's hand in marriage on Erast. Leander's steward Bartholomew (*The Celebrant*) does all he can to keep his master out of debt, and conspires with Leander's uncle to rid his master of the toadies and hangers-on who have been his ruin. The pert lady's maid Jadwiga (Eleonora's maid in *The Litigant*) flirts with Figlacki (Leander's valet), and both conspire to further the courtship of their master and mistress. Here again Figlacki (who does not hesitate to eavesdrop if it is to his master's advantage) pretends to be someone else in order to deceive the litigator. Another Jadwiga (*The Satirist*) flirts with Filutowicz (Trickster), the valet of Obmowski —while the unhappy lot of valets in eighteenth-century Poland (they were drawn from the peasantry) is illustrated by the way Obmowski orders him to and fro, and even strikes him.

The gallery is completed by other familiar figures: fashionable ladies (*The Celebrant*), a drunkard (*ibid.*), a corrupt lawyer (*The Litigant*), the self-styled "philosophers" (*The Politician*) who are nothing more than tricksters and charlatans.

II *Technique*

Like all playwrights of the eighteenth century, Krasicki was a firm believer in the "unities" and other rules governing dramaturgy. Like his contemporaries all over Europe and Russia, he thought that observance of the "unities" added to a play's verisimilitude, and that it was absurd not to observe them (one of Shakespeare's "faults" was that he failed to do so).

Of the three unities (as understood by playwrights), the most important appears to have been that of "time." It was also the easiest to observe, requiring only that the action of a play be completed within a given length of time (from three to 24 hours). Playwrights had several ways of indicating the passage of time in their plays: characters might inquire what time it was, clocks could chime, or meals be served at appropriate times. The function of these devices was to draw the attention of the audience to the fact that the playwright was observing the "unity of time" in his play.

There were also less obvious ways of observing the rules. One, forgotten since the rules fell into disuse, was concerned with the interval between acts—used in eighteenth-century dramaturgy for disposing of "time to be lost," when events not sufficiently interesting or dramatic to be shown on the stage might be supposed to have taken place. Krasicki uses a convention that indicates *no* lapse of time had occurred between the end of one act and the start of the next, when he depicts the same character appearing in the last scene of an act, and in the first scene of the next. To an audience familiar with the rules, this indicated that no time had been "lost" in the interval.

Characters entered or left the stage in accordance with other rules or formulae, which provided them with reasons for appearing or going out. A basic rule was that the stage must never be left empty (this meant the act was ended): at least one person must be present, delivering a monologue. Plausible reasons for a character to enter included the "search" formula, when an actor would declare he was looking for another character. The "inquiry" formula was also acceptable, when a character appeared on stage to find out what was happening (after a noisy brawl, for example).

Entrances were usually preceded by a character already on stage announcing "I see him coming!", "Here is my husband—very apropos!" or the like. Such remarks served two purposes: they helped the audience identify the new character, and also gave the cue for the actor about to appear. Little is known of the stages for which Krasicki's comedies were written, but it seems likely that they resembled most European stages of the period in being long and deep, rather than wide. This meant that characters entered from the rear and proceeded towards the footlights in order to take up their cues. Consequently the audience would see the character whose entry was being announced.

Other formulae were used to provide cues for exits. "Flight" from another character was always a useful pretext, or characters might announce that they had to change clothes, write a letter, attend to business, or eat dinner.

Still more rules governed the division of plays into acts and scenes. What are believed to be his first and last comedies[3]—*The Satirist* and *The Litigant*—are both in five acts (the classical number). The others are divided into three acts, an acceptable division for the comparatively low genre of comedy.

As always in classical dramaturgy, a new scene begins whenever a new character enters. Although the number of scenes to an act was not fixed, Krasicki evidently realized that a large number of short scenes helped make a play livelier and faster-moving when it was produced on the stage than a play with fewer, longer scenes. So *The Politician,* although it has only three acts, contains fifty scenes, as compared to the slower-moving *Litigant,* with five acts but only forty-four scenes.

A feature of eighteenth-century comedy which Krasicki introduces frequently is the monologue, in which a character, left alone on the stage, talks to himself (for the benefit of the audience). The monologue was a useful device which helped playwrights observe the rule that the stage must never be left empty until the end of an act. *The Celebrant* begins with an expository monologue by the servant Bartholomew, who explains the situation and refers to characters that are about to appear. In *The Politician* it is the sensible raisonneur who delivers the opening monologue, expatiating on the folly of "Cogitator." But for all the practical value of monologues, Krasicki shared the view of many eighteenth-century playwrights that the device (like the "aside") was artificial. This is apparent by the frequency with which other characters, upon entering, ask the character delivering the monologue why he is talking to himself.

III *Local Color*

The comedies discussed above are examples of the "comedy of character," as witness the satirical attacks on the follies and vices of mankind in general. The play *The Embroidery Frame* (originally known as *In the Fashionable Manner*) comes closer to the "comedy of manners," which deals not so much with the vices and follies of all mankind, but with affectations and follies of contemporary society. To be sure the playwrights' main purpose in both kinds of comedy was always to expose stupidities and urge the improvement of society; but in the comedy of manners stronger emphasis falls on contemporary aspects.

The Embroidery Frame has almost no intrigue to speak of, but within its brief scope, Krasicki presents a range of characters who (even though they are caricatures) provide an amusing picture of eighteenth-century Polish society. Mrs. Lubska, a Warsaw "co-quette," descends upon the rural household of Mr. and Mrs. Spokojski ("Tranquil"), and their two daughters. Mrs. Lubska is a prototype of Mickiewicz's Telimena (*Pan Tadeusz,* 1834): she uses rouge "to correct nature," declares she has a box at the Warsaw theater merely "to see and be seen," is bored by the countryside, and intrigues with the fop Wiatrakowski ("Wind-Mill") against the play's virtuous and sensible hero. Wiatrakowski, on his part, is a fashionable young man who speaks French beautifully, but Polish not very well, and boasts of having visited England. He is accompanied by absurd gallants and fops. Mr. "Tranquil's" elder daughter reads romances and believes in dreams. In addition, Krasicki offers thumb-nail character sketches of Mr. "Tranquil's" neighbor, Rubasiewicz ("Mr. Coarse") with his hunting dogs, fondness for Hungarian wine, and talkative wife.

Krasicki's comedies of character also included items of local color. After all, Krasicki had to make clear to his audiences that they themselves were the object of his satire, and this could best be done by surrounding the characters with familiar scenes of everyday life in eighteenth-century Poland. So characters are seen reading the Warsaw newspaper, complaining of the high cost of postal services in Poland, or of bribery in the Lublin courts, referring to current political events, to annual fairs held throughout the country, Polish money, all kinds of now-forgotten food and drink, or articles of dress—even the "beauty spots" made of black silk and worn by ladies to bring out the whiteness of their complexion.

Krasicki's comedies are never performed today, though they would make diverting *jeux d'esprit* if given, perhaps, in the Orangery at Heilsberg, for which Krasicki wrote several of them. Yet, though we are not likely to see his plays performed, they reveal yet another facet of his lively and ceaselessly productive mind, and should be considered in any survey of his creative work.

CHAPTER 10

Theory and Practice of Poetry

DURING the last decade of his life, Krasicki was generally recognized by contemporary writers and literary theorists in Poland as the most eminent authority on literature. He owed his prestige to the wide range of his own work, and to his engagement in the campaign for enlightenment in literature, criticism and society. But Krasicki demonstrated his critical interest in poetry throughout his career, beginning as early as 1766 with an article in the *Monitor* (no. 24). Here, he insisted that "all kinds of writing (including poetry) should be clear, easily understood, well-ordered, more natural than artificial." He was, of course, using the key-word "natural" in the eighteenth-century sense, as that which is the opposite of "abnormal," and was following in the footsteps of the ubiquitous Horace. Krasicki was hostile to the poetry of the Polish Baroque Period (1600–1750), especially in its later manifestations. His complaint of the "conceits, allusions to coats-of-arms, involved allegories and monstrous metaphors" in which this poetry abounds is almost an echo of Dr. Johnson's celebrated remarks on the poetry of Cowley and the English Metaphysicals, in which "the most heterogeneous ideas are yoked by violence together; nature and art are ransacked for illustrations, comparisons and allusions." [1]

Krasicki appears to have planned a *Craft of Versifying*, but it was never published, and we do not even know whether he actually wrote it. Nevertheless, the mere fact that he should have considered composing such a work indicated his interest in the theoretical and technical aspects of his art. Like a number of his contemporaries in the Age of Enlightenment, Krasicki believed it was his duty to contribute to the works of literary theory produced in that period, and during the last ten years of his life he composed his *On Versifying and Versifiers* (1793–1801, published posthumously in 1803). The work is a kind of encyclopedia, biographical dictionary and anthology rolled into one, and in it Krasicki ranges widely through world literature (as it was then understood), from the Bible, the literatures of classical Greece and Rome and the literatures of Europe to the poetry of Persia, Arabia and China. One country whose poetry he did not consider was Russia, and in other cases his remarks border on the perfunctory (e.g. the literature of Spain is condensed into a single page).

If *On Versifying* provides little information that is of value today, we should bear in mind the public to which Krasicki addressed it. *On Versifying* is essentially a work of "popularization," not intended for poets or literary historians, but for people who were interested in poetry, and wanted to know more about the topic. For present-day readers, the work is of most interest as a yard-stick of Krasicki's own tastes in literature, which can be measured by what he has to say of certain authors, and by the amount of space he devotes to them.

Predictably, Homer and Virgil are well represented: Horace is described as "the poet one can never have too much of," and Krasicki provides a long summary of Aristotle's *Poetics*. Although Tibullus and Catullus only rate a few lines, Lucan is awarded a long quotation. Among the Italian poets, Dante, Tasso and Metastasio are well represented, as are Boileau, Gresset, Delille and Voltaire in French. Krasicki's favorite German poets were Gellert, Klopstock and Gessner (whose insipid idylls enjoyed considerable vogue and influence in late eighteenth-century poetry all over Europe). He refers to Chaucer as "the English Homer," a remark that suggests Krasicki never read him: indeed, it would be remarkable if he had, since most if not all of Krasicki's knowledge of English literature appears to have been acquired through French translations. Alexander Pope is said to "occupy a high place among the first poets of England," and is represented by a lengthy extract from *The Rape of the Lock*, translated into Polish by J. U. Niemcewicz. Krasicki also had a high opinion of the "bardic poetry" of Ossian (which he believed genuine, and of which he translated portions).

Predictably, too, Shakespeare's plays aroused mixed feelings in Krasicki: although the plays "sometimes contain expressions worthy of the greatest amazement," Krasicki considers that Shakespeare was "unequal in flight, often exaggerating by excess of effort, while sometimes sinking so low that it is hardly credible

that such differences should occur in the work of the same writer."
The plays "breathe a sort of wildness and have the brand of their
period, although amidst the worst errors there sometimes appear
lights that elevate their writer above all others." Krasicki much
preferred Addison as a playwright, and devotes three times as
much space to him as to Shakespeare, accompanying his remarks
with a translated passage from the tragedy *Cato*. Nor did Krasicki
entirely approve of Milton's *Paradise Lost*, though he admits that
"despite the criticism it deserves, the work enjoys fame and
honor."

Part IV of *On Versifying* is concerned with Polish literature,
which begins (for Krasicki) before 1000 A.D. with the well-
known poem "Dei Genetrix," (Mother of God) addressed to the
Virgin Mary. Krasicki includes the work of sixteenth-century
poets writing in Latin as an integral part of Polish literature, and
devotes space to the "father of Polish poetry," Rej, whom he rec-
ognizes as the "first poet to write in his native language." For all
his well-attested admiration for Jan Kochanowski (1530–1584),
Krasicki feels obliged to make certain reservations when describing Kochanowski's *Epigrams*, which contain "thoughts and expressions" that should not have been permitted.

Proceeding chronologically, Krasicki quotes with approval the
Latin poetry and idylls of Szymon Szymonowicz (1558–1629),
better known by the Latinized form of his name as Simonides.
The literary genre of the idyll (which has its roots in classical
antiquity with Theocritus) entered Polish poetry through the
idylls of Simonides, published in 1614, and continued to flourish
until reaching its climax in Mickiewicz's *Pan Tadeusz* (1834).[2]
Another Polish poet whose Latin poetry was known in Western
Europe (as was the Latin poetry of Simonides) was Sarbiewski,
to whom Krasicki next turns his attention, providing biographical
details and a Polish version of one of Sarbiewski's better-known
lyrics.

After passing rapidly over the Baroque poets (of whom he men-
tions only Kochowski, Twardowski, Potocki, Zimorowic and the
Morsztyns—without committing himself to any critical evaluation
of their poetry), Krasicki reaches the Saxon period, represented
chiefly by Elizabeth Druzbacka (1693–1765). One of Poland's
first female poets, Druzbacka has recently been the subject of revived interest.[3] The survey ends with a brief note on his contem-

porary, Bishop Naruszewicz, whose works are however "too well known to be included here." In accordance with eighteenth-century reticence, Krasicki has not a word to say of his own poetry.

I *The* Chocim War

Krasicki believed an epic poem to be the greatest work of which human nature is capable. In his *On Versifying*, he placed this genre well to the forefront of the various kinds, and himself turned to the epic of 1781 with the *Chocim War*. The poem was "written to order" in support of King Stanislas August's abortive political plans of an alliance between Poland and Russia against the Turks, and with this purpose in mind, Krasicki went back to a celebrated battle at Chocim (1621), a locality then in Moldavia, where an army of Polish troops supported by Cossacks had defeated twice their number of Turks under the ambitious Sultan Osman II. For the heroic central figure which epic poetry required, Krasicki selected the Hetman Chodkiewicz, whose deeds on the battle-field of Chocim had been celebrated in a Baroque epic by Waclaw Potocki (1670), bearing the same title as Krasicki's. However, it is most unlikely that Krasicki knew Potocki's "monotonous account of important and unimportant events in the trenches of Chocim," which "cannot claim a particularly high place in the hierarchy of European poetry," [4] since it remained in manuscript until 1850, and in any case Krasicki would certainly not have admired his predecessor's Baroque conceits, digressions (often the most poetical passages) and lack of form.

Krasicki's epic consists of twelve cantos, though for an epic his poem is on the small side (just over 2000 lines, as compared to ten thousand lines in the *Aeneid*). All the same, he took as his models the two epics most widely admired in eighteenth-century Europe: Virgil's *Aeneid* and Voltaire's *Henriade,* which went into some sixty editions during its author's lifetime, and which follows the Latin poem closely. [5]

Krasicki's *Chocim War* is stiff with poetic diction, and he was careful to insert all the components of classical epic he had derided in *The Battle of Mice* only six years earlier. Heroic similes, references to elevated mythological beings, catalogs of high-sounding names and a splendid funeral all have their place. But despite its correctness, the poem is generally left unread. Even Krasicki's contemporaries failed to show much interest in it, despite Krasicki's popularity as a writer and the highly patriotic content of the narrative.

The truth is that Krasicki wrote the poem to order for King Stanislas, but his heart clearly was not in the task. Though Krasicki was the major Polish writer of his century and a master of his own language, with a poetic technique (of an eighteenth-century kind) rarely if ever surpassed, he had no feeling for those elements that make up a genuine epic (nor did Voltaire, despite the popularity of the *Henriade*). Being enlightened men, neither Krasicki nor Voltaire was able to draw upon the symbolic sources of myth from which true epics come. Lacking this, Krasicki tried to compensate by casting his tone too high, with the result that the poem is high-pitched, slightly but unmistakably absurd.

II *Songs of Ossian*

James Macpherson's flamboyant prose-poems entitled *The Poems of Ossian* (1765) were one of the most notorious literary hoaxes ever perpetrated on an unwitting public. Not that everyone was taken in: Dr. Johnson saw through the hoax and remarked of the "poems" that "a man might write such stuff forever, if he would abandon his mind to it." [6] Yet the *Poems* became widely popular, and were soon translated into French and German.

Krasicki presumably believed the *Poems* were genuine, though this is not the point. What is surprising is that he was sufficiently interested in the work to translate it into Polish. Ossian's poems, with their apparently spontaneous and primitive tone, were a harbinger of the Romantic movement, and expressed a growing revolt throughout Europe against Classicism. Their literary value was minimal, but their influence and significance were considerable—and Krasicki perceived this.

Unfortunately his version was based on a French rendering,[7] in hexameters, so that Krasicki's Ossianic poems (following the French instead of the rhythmical prose of the original) are in eleven-syllable couplets. Ossian's poems, after all, purported to be only a prose version of ancient Celtic poetry, and the fact that Macpherson's "renditions" escaped the bonds of metrical conformity to which an eighteenth-century ear was accustomed was one of the reasons why the poems proved such a startling novelty. Yet

Krasicki's decision to translate the poems indicates yet again his far-ranging and cosmopolitan literary interests, his insight into the literary trends of Western Europe, and his determination to bring what he considered the best in European literature into Polish culture.

III   *Verse and Prose*

Krasicki composed a number of "miscellaneous" and "occasional" poems which appeared at various times in magazines, anthologies or as pamphlets. A collection of these fugitive pieces was published in Warsaw as *Letters and Miscellaneous Writings of His Grace the Bishop of Warmia* (I, 1786, II, 1788). They range from odes and hymns, idylls and songs, to epitaphs and verbal jokes, and cover a wide variety of topics.

Yet for all their variety, the presence of two great literary figures is to be felt throughout the collection: Horace and Kochanowski.[8] Indeed, the longest compositions in the collection look back directly to Horace, and include the description of a visit to the "beloved homestead of Kochanowski." These are the "Journey away from Warsaw," and its counterpart, the "Journey back to Warsaw." "Journey" poems were a favorite genre in eighteenth-century poetry (Krasicki's contemporaries Karpinski and Zablocki composed such poems), and the genre itself derives from Horace's Satire I, 5, known as "Iter Brindisium" (Voyage to Brindisi). However, Krasicki's compositions differ from the others in that they are structured on a narrative prose "thread," into which the versified fragments are set at intervals. Both his "journey" poems are addressed to Prince Stanislas Poniatowski.

Krasicki's journeys resemble Horace's journey to Brindisium in that neither poet was particularly interested in the natural beauties of the landscapes through which their routes led. Both were more concerned with the company they kept, the accommodations provided, and man-made objects along the way: houses, gardens, churches and the like. Throughout, the tone is light, and Krasicki's easy familiarity with his addressee gives the accounts of his journeys a pleasing grace.

Czarnolas (the "beloved homestead of Kochanowski"), which Krasicki briefly visits during the first journey, provides the occasion for a poem into which he introduces neat references to the celebrated linden tree in whose shade the poet used to sing, to the "Saint John's Eve" cycle of pastoral poems, and to the *Laments* Kochanowski wrote on the death of his daughter.

Krasicki's "adoration" (as he called it) of Kochanowski and his poetry is understandable. For two centuries Kochanowski's poetry had been the supreme artistic achievement in Polish literature, generally recognized as a model of poetic excellence.[9] After all, Kochanowski's poetry had brought the classical art of Renaissance Humanism into Poland. Then again, the spirit of Horace is never far from Kochanowski's poetry, and this was certain to add to his stature in the eyes of Krasicki. But Kochanowski's major contribution to Polish poetry was his success in transforming the language itself into a flexible and artistic means of expression by purifying the vernacular of the crudeness of medieval writers. Krasicki was engaged in a similar task—that of purifying his native language of the debased forms that had infiltrated into it during the late Baroque period. Pope's cult of Milton and Spenser came from a similar source.

The collection of "miscellaneous poems" has been rearranged into chronological order by its present-day editors,[10] though Krasicki is known to have drawn up a list of the order in which he wanted the poems printed. However, his own editor (Dmochowski) changed this order, so it is not possible at this time to be sure that Krasicki was following the Horatian principle of ordering his poems to imply contrast between them and thus to achieve variety.

Most of the topics with which the poems deal are familiar from Krasicki's other writings: he rails against the depravity of the present ("We have lost both Virtue and our State," and "The homeland, once overflowing/ With treasure, arms and virtue,/ Today is in a different condition"), and praises "olden times," when "the young respected the old, and there were no spendthrifts, bankrupts or cheats." The constant ups-and-downs of Fortune in men's lives engage Krasicki's thoughts, as they had engaged those of Horace. Disapproval of court life, with its flattery, deception and sycophancy, is an ever-present theme. Characteristically, Krasicki (again following Horace and Kochanowski) shows a marked preference for rural retirement, where he can meditate on the "golden mean," recommend moderation in all things, and urge a Stoic endurance of whatever Fate brings.

Most of Krasicki's poems in the collection are odes, a poetic genre that enjoyed considerable prestige in the eighteenth century as a result of its association with Horace and other classical poets. Odes are poems addressed to someone else (or to an abstract concept, or even to an object), and they were often composed for a special occasion, on which they were recited aloud. Krasicki's odes have a range of addressees, ranging from God to friends and relatives, and down to "Delightful thicket!" and a laurel bush.

Generally speaking, Krasicki's poems and odes are pleasing and ingenious, and bring us closer to the poet himself than any of his other work—with one exception, and that is his private correspondence, to which we next turn.

CHAPTER 11

Familiar Letters

LETTER-writing as a minor literary genre in its own right flourished all over Europe in the eighteenth century, as it had flourished in Imperial Rome under the emperor Augustus. It was cultivated just as the art of conversation was cultivated—to display elegance and wit without stiffness or formality. But many eminent persons of the period also wrote familiar letters with at least one eye on possible publication: this manner of proceeding became fashionable after the widespread success of Mme. de Sevigné's letters (published posthumously in 1724). Voltaire's letters were published, as were those of the Earl of Shaftesbury, Lord Chesterfield and Lady Wortley-Montagu. The practice looked back to Imperial Rome and the publication of Cicero's letters.

A handful of Krasicki's letters was published by Gröll in Warsaw (1786), but Krasicki complained that they had been published without his knowledge (his secretary is believed to have sold them to Gröll without his master's permission). The incident remains somewhat mysterious even today, and is remarkably reminiscent of the "curious intrigue" whereby Alexander Pope obtained the publication of his letters, without appearing implicated.[1] That Krasicki was well aware of the practice is made evident by his remarks in 1777:

It is laid down, my dear Count, that our letters open with reproaches and end with expressions of affection. If some day anyone takes it into his head to publish them, our readers—accustomed to this preamble—will skip gracefully over the avant-propos.

However, we have had to wait until the present for the publication of Krasicki's collected letters, as is the case with other eighteenth-century Polish literary men such as Naruszewicz, Trembecki and Karpiński.

We now have access to a total of over 700 of Krasicki's letters, as well as a number from his correspondents. They cover the period from 1744 to 1801, and their range is wide: from letters on matters connected with the Church and official business, to letters of condolence and compliment. All the ingredients found in his poetry and prose reappear in the letters, including wit, irony, urbanity and a little misanthropy. But we look in vain for penetrating revelations of self, and if Krasicki was haunted (as was his contemporary Dr. Johnson) by "intermittent glances into a dark world," [2] he never says so. In reading Krasicki's letters, it is fitting to bear in mind Dr. Johnson's comments on the letters of Pope: "It has been so long said as to be commonly believed, that the true characters of men may be found in their letters, and that he who writes to his friend lays his heart open before him . . ."—a notion which Dr. Johnson then proceeded to demolish, by adding: "There is indeed no transaction which offers stronger temptations to fallacy and sophistication (i.e. lying) than epistolary intercourse." Far from being the most open and "sincere" literary form, the familiar letter is perhaps one of the least so.

Krasicki's correspondents included two crowned heads of Europe: Stanislas Augustus and Frederick of Prussia. But the bulk of his letters was addressed to three persons: his younger brother Antoni (born 1735), who lived most of his life on the Krasicki family estate in south-east Poland, became a country gentleman fond of hunting, eating and drinking, and was later afflicted with the aristocratic ailment of gout; Count Lehndorff (1727–1811), whom Krasicki first met in Berlin in 1769 during a visit to the court of Frederick, and with whom he maintained a correspondence for some thirty years; and Kajetan Ghigiotti, a Church dignitary, who was born in Naples but spent many years as head of the Italian department of the Cabinet in Warsaw, and who obtained honorary Polish citizenship in 1768. He preceded Krasicki in death in 1796.

The letters Krasicki wrote to these three individuals vary considerably: the tone in the letters to his younger brother is often almost paternal, and they are full of benevolent or anxious inquiries as to the health and well-being of his brother and the rest of

the family, with requests for news of the family estate and local
gossip. Addressing Count Lehndorff, Krasicki reveals himself as
an urbane, well-read and witty aristocrat, familiar with the ways
of the world and rationally skeptical about them. The letters to
Ghigiotti are again different, being a shade less formal, and concerned with such mundane preoccupations as the acquisition of
Church benefices, items of gossip from the court in Warsaw, and
requests for the dispatch of books, wine or chocolate from the
capital. Throughout the correspondence, it is clear that his friend-
ships with Lehndorff and Ghigiotti meant a great deal to Krasicki,
though the letters (which are in French or occasionally Italian)
retain a characteristically light-hearted tone with a touch of formality—Krasicki addresses Lehndorff as "vous," or "mon cher
comte" at all times. But he was not above calling Ghigiotti such
facetious names as "Cardinal Frangipani" or "Mandarin."

Although "rules" existed for the composition of letters—as they
did for the other kinds of literature—Krasicki would have none of
them. He dismissed the two best-known writers of "methods" for
composing letters as "forced," and on one occasion slyly warns a
correspondent that he intends to make his present letter "the shal-
lowest of all letters written since the times of Balzac and Voiture,"* whose letters were regarded in their own day as models of
good taste and decorum. On the other hand, Krasicki had a high
regard for the "quiet informality" of the letters of Cicero, which
had been published and republished all over Europe since their
discovery in the fourteenth century. Krasicki admired the
"smoothness of style and conciseness of expression" in Cicero's
correspondence. He also held in high esteem the letters of Mme.
de Sevigné, which he placed above all others for their "charm." As
he confided to Lehndorff, he was unable to put her letters down,
once he started to read them; his own letters abound in references
and allusions to hers, and he possessed a bust representing the
lady. His admiration is not surprising, since Krasicki himself possessed something of Mme. de Sevigné's genius for the writing of
familiar letters, as witness the manner in which he instinctively
adopted a tone and style that suited the character of his various
addressees; he could be witty and light-hearted, or sympathetic

---

* Jean Louis Guez de Balzac, French writer, 1594–1654; Vincent
Voiture, French poet and man of letters, 1597–1648.

and understanding, or "literary" (as in his letters to Stanislas Augustus, where the style is formal, dignified, but never servile). As he said, his cardinal principle in writing a letter was to "avoid boring" his reader.

I *The Art of Enjoyment*

The letters give an intimate picture (by eighteenth-century standards) of Krasicki's way of life at the Bishop's Palace in Heilsberg, where he lived from 1767 until his elevation to the Archbishopric of Gniezno in 1795. The letters demonstrate one of the most pervasive concerns of Augustan thought—that an enlightened man should pattern his daily life in accordance with "taste, nature and reason." This was not an age when men sought to perform heroic deeds on a battlefield or to achieve salvation in the next world. Like many of his contemporaries all over Europe, Krasicki was interested in creating a civilized context for living and writing, but not very much in anything else.

A substantial part of the Bishop's Palace was built in the "Gothic" style, and Krasicki (true to his eighteenth-century tastes) found it "rude and primitive," "a tumble-down old place." Gothic architecture, after all, evoked the scorn of many Classicists, and had been disparaged in the *Tatler* and *Spectator*. Krasicki also derided the growing taste for "artificial ruins" associated with the "Gothic." When he visited an "immense edifice" in the shape of an "Ionic and Corinthian ruin," erected on the orders of a certain Count Los, he dismissed it as "the most absurd thing in the world." Yet Krasicki's dislike of ruins was founded on a rational premise: as he said in 1782, "I have seen too many genuine ruins in Poland, and am disgusted forever with this species of monument."

Fortunately there was also a modern part to the Palace, and here Krasicki had his apartments and library. The palace boasted a garden too, which he made particularly his own. He introduced an "English-style garden," and invited Lehndorff to visit it, so they might hold "great discussions on the subject of plantations, promenades, temples, kiosks, bridges, alleys." The garden was adorned with tablets commemorating the memory of departed friends, each with an epitaph composed by Krasicki. The vogue for "English gardens," which marked a reaction against the symmetry and geometrically shaped regularity of Renaissance and seventeenth-century garden landscaping, constitutes an extension of the bounds of taste, and Krasicki's contribution to this extension should not be overlooked. He was especially proud of the orangery, where he could stroll in winter, and where plays were sometimes staged for the delectation of friends and neighbors.

By 1777 Krasicki was well established at Heilsberg, and could describe his life as follows:

What do I do? I do nothing, or, as my friend La Fontaine once said, I do 'nothings.' But thanks to my happy disposition, I resist contagion, and am not bored. Some friends, my books, my study, my card-game —these take up three-quarters of the day, and at night I sleep without dreams—or if I dream, 'tis not of the devil.

His plans for that summer included the "cultivation of cabbages and of wisdom."

Eating and drinking occupied a substantial part of Krasicki's time: he was particularly anxious to engage a cook from the household of the late Hetman Branicki, and for some years employed a German cook, though when the latter departed, Krasicki employed a Pole in his kitchen and boasted that "we are now eating twice as well and more appetizingly than before." He looks forward to the arrival of another cook from Warsaw, who must be able to serve Polish dishes: "sausage, puddings, dumplings, beet-root soup, bouillon and the like." Wine figures in many letters: before visiting his brother Antoni, Krasicki asks that he should lay in "Burgundy wine—not strong, but genuine, such as I always drink." If Burgundy is not to be had, Krasicki advises his brother that he would be glad to drink a local wine. Later he advises him that "your Hungarian wine, especially when old, is not to my taste." On his elevation to the Archbishopric of Gniezno, Krasicki celebrated the occasion by ordering "six barrels of white Hungarian table-wine . . . even if a small barrel should cost as much as twenty-five or thirty *zlotys.*"

Social life at Heilsberg was not lacking. Krasicki celebrated his "name day" in 1781 "splendidly, noisily, joyously," with over a hundred guests at the Palace, and libations to match. On the birthday of the King of Prussia in 1782 he reports dining with forty persons, where the "trumpets played so well that we were almost deafened." "Carnival" was celebrated with balls: in 1786 he writes of attending a "masked ball" on Tuesday, a "gala" on Sunday and a sleigh-party and another masked ball on Monday, though he confides in Lehndorff that while the festivities were not "superb or magnificent, yet they were animated and joyous." Carnival in 1790 ended with a "masked ball in Town," and another which Krasicki himself gave, where "the quadrilles were very elegant." He also visited the Court of Frederick at Potsdam as a welcome guest dining with the king, attending theaters, operas, balls and fashionable "routs." However, he can also look back from the crowded city to the "charms of my solitude" at Heilsberg.

Yet Krasicki's sojourn at Heilsberg was not as idyllic as his frequent references to eating and drinking, card-playing, gardening, reading and amateur theatricals might make it seem. As a genuinely and deeply patriotic Pole, living in former Polish territories occupied by the Prussians, Krasicki was well aware that he was an exile, even in solitude. He was unable to leave his diocese without the express permission of Frederick, and he speaks wryly of himself as a "hermit" in a "Prussian Kamchatka," or "buried in the full sense of that word." In 1779 he tells Ghigiotti that "far from my homeland, relatives and friends, my only consolation is in the letters I receive from Poland." He complains that "on the shores of the Baltic, one gradually loses the ways of the world." He thanks Lehndorff for not neglecting "the most retired of hermits," and speaks of himself in another letter to the same correspondent as "a poor hermit sadly vegetating in a dilapidated old castle."

Krasicki's letters abound in ironically plaintive references to money troubles and debts. This situation was common enough in Poland of that day: even Stanislas Augustus himself was chronically in debt, obliged to borrow money where he could, and to accept Russian funds to gratify his expensive tastes. Krasicki was debt-ridden for most of his ecclesiastical career, though this state of affairs was not entirely his own fault: he had to keep up appearances as "His Grace the Bishop of Warmia," and after 1772 (the First Partition), Frederick's administrators took to confiscating half of the income of the Catholic Church. This explains Krasicki's repeated efforts to acquire a greater income—not crowned with success, however, until 1795.

His writing, of course, brought him nothing but fame. His War-

saw publisher "paid" him with copies of books, and his most popular works were shamelessly pirated. But literature was still a
financially unrewarding profession in eighteenth-century Poland.

II   *The Observer*

The eighteenth century was an age of unparalleled turbulence
all over Europe, and as early as 1760 (when in Rome) Krasicki
reported to his brother that "here in Italy we are probably to have
war. The Spanish army has landed close to Genoa, the Sardinians
are under arms, 25,000 Neapolitans are stationed not far from the
Papal frontiers." These alarming incidents were connected with
the expulsion of the Jesuit order from countries then ruled by the
Bourbon dynasty.

Krasicki played only a minor part in the 1768 Confederation of
Bar, an armed uprising by Poles directed against Russian intervention.[3] This event, which started in Podolia and the Ukraine,
soon spread across Poland and resulted in four years of guerilla
warfare that almost cost Stanislas Augustus his throne and fore-
shadowed the coming decline and fall of the Polish state.

The year 1772 (along with the year 1939) has rightly been described as "among the blackest of modern times . . . the dis-
memberment of Poland was the suicide of the old Europe." [4] Although Krasicki never concerned himself overmuch with politics,
he was astute enough to perceive this, and he—along with many
of his enlightened contemporaries—realized to the full the dan-
gers lurking in the First Partition. He was affected by it person-
ally, after all: when it was rumored that Prussia was about to
annex the Polish province of Warmia (the seat of his own bishopric) in June 1772, he appealed to Pope Clement XIV to prevent
the annexation. But the appeal was of no avail. Krasicki's own
bishopric was seized by the Prussians shortly afterwards, though
he remained its bishop.

Krasicki's comments on political events become increasingly
skeptical, even cynical, as one disaster followed another, and Poland, once a powerful and important European state, gradually
became a victim to external and internal discord, greed and strug-
gles for power of a most unedifying kind. His reaction to the
"Great Diet" of 1788 was characteristic: this Diet aroused great
interest and intense anxiety, and led to the introduction by Stanislas Augustus of a new constitution which the English statesman

Burke praised in a noble eulogy. The constitution was, in effect, an attempt to transform Poland's medieval and antiquated system into a constitutional monarchy of modern type. It also made Catherine the Great very angry. Krasicki, however, dismissed it as a "charivari," and saw fit to quote the proverb "the more it thunders, the less it rains."

When the Diet deliberated an increase in taxation on the Church, his comment was "Poland is arming . . . and the unfortunate clergy pay the piper." By June 1792 he was resigned to what he called a "visit" by Russian troops to put down the 1791 Constitution, and abolish the reforms. His attitude is best expressed by a description of himself busy in his garden "not paying any attention to the war," and looking forward to a "crowded and amusing winter" with a regiment of the Prussian army garrisoned in Heilsberg. The officers took part in amateur theatricals at the Palace. When the Kościuszko insurrection (the final struggle for Polish independence) broke out in April 1794, accompanied by the hanging of several eminent pro-Russian dignitaries (including a Bishop), Krasicki coolly remarks that "it is not very nice." When more executions took place in June that year, Krasicki urges his correspondent: "Let us be merry, despite everything that is happening." After his elevation to the Archbishopric of Gniezno, Krasicki ceased referring to political matters: nor did he refer to the unfortunate Stanislas Augustus, whose reign ended in bankruptcy, humiliation, exile and death in Russia.

III *Quotations and Allusions*

"A quotation never harmed a letter," wrote Krasicki, citing Corneille. Other writers whose works evidently constituted part of the "furniture" of Krasicki's mind included his "good friend Horace." He also quoted from Rabelais and other French writers—La Fontaine, Boileau, Molière, Voltaire—while of Polish authors, Jan Kochanowski could always be relied upon to provide a quotation. True to his eighteenth-century standards of taste, Krasicki never quoted pedantically: his quotations imply that his correspondent will catch the relevance of the allusion which, in turn, functions largely as a simile or metaphor in providing an insight into a writer's mind.

CHAPTER 12

Conclusion

P OPE and Voltaire have been frequently mentioned in this study. To be sure, there were considerable differences in personality between these two writers and Krasicki: Krasicki was never as priggish, spiteful and vindictive as Pope, nor as malicious and highly-strung as Voltaire. Yet all three shared certain views and opinions. They regarded poetry as an "art"—the "art" of making poetry, in much the same way that a composer like Johann Sebastian Bach "made" a concerto, or Chippendale "made" a chair. They, and most of their contemporaries, believed that sense and reason are as indispensable in poetry as they are in any other form of human activity. All three were "enlightened" in every meaning of that word—except for one: they were not enlightened psychologically. For all the wit, irony, perfection of form in their writings, theirs is not poetry that extends the confines of the human spirit. Eighteenth-century poets did not set out to do so. Nevertheless, it seems likely that this fact is the greatest barrier to enjoyment and understanding when we approach eighteenth-century literature today.

Writers of the Age of Enlightenment, strongly influenced though many of them were by the ideas of Hobbes, Locke and other "rationalist" philosophers (to the effect that the "imagination" was something closely akin to madness and must therefore be kept in restraint or suppressed altogether), were not entirely unaware of the irrational aspects of man's nature. They denounced and ridiculed such manifestations of the irrational as a belief in ghosts, spirits, witches or dreams. Yet the period is marked by a number of poets and others who sooner or later came into conflict with the "irrational" in their own psyches, and who suffered in consequence from fits of melancholia (Dr. Johnson), madness (John Clare, Kniaznin) or suicide (Chatterton).[1] Not until a new generation arrived (with the Romantics) did dreams and ghosts enter into poetry, as writers began using precisely these manifestations to explore the "mysterious way that leads inwards," into the poet's unconscious. Their voyages of exploration were often made in literary forms that were equally alien to the eighteenth century—huge, unfinished dramas, "fragments," "improvisations" and the like. In the eighteenth century, poetry was a conscious activity, confined within rational boundaries—though both Krasicki and Pope succeeded on occasion in escaping into a realm of fantasy in the *Battle of Mice* and *The Rape of the Lock*, respectively.

Again, eighteenth-century poets and their readers were spiritually and mentally closer to the writers of Imperial Rome than they are to us. The all-pervasive presence of Horace in eighteenth-century poetry has already been mentioned here. Classical and mythological allusions provide further evidence of the communality and powerful links felt between eighteenth-century writers and classical antiquity. Of course, footnotes can provide us with clues to such allusions in the poetry of Pope or Krasicki: but footnotes lack the resonance these allusions possessed two hundred years ago. Indeed, it is no exaggeration to suggest that the classical allusions which abound in European poetry, until the Romantics discarded them, performed a function similar to that performed by such devices as imagery, metaphor, ambiguity and association in the poetry of today.

Venus, Cupid, Mars and the assorted nymphs and satyrs who populate much eighteenth-century poetry are undoubtedly another barrier to our understanding. For, as Professor Sutherland has shown, they had by that time become little more than "contractions," [2] which poets used instead of describing at length. When every stream is a "naiad," how is the poet to differentiate between one stream and another? Most eighteenth-century poets did not consider it their business to do so. We, conditioned by the great Romantics from Wordsworth to Mickiewicz and Pushkin, tend to believe—rightly or wrongly—that it was.

The Augustan spirit was something Krasicki possessed along with all the major eighteenth-century writers. It has been defined by Ian Watt (with reference to English literature) as a special way of thinking and writing, marked by "precise syntax, elegant diction, very detached in its attitude both to subject and audience." [3] Irony—"speaking by contraries"—was characteristic of this way of thinking and writing.

Like the other great ironists of that age (Swift, Pope, Gibbon, Voltaire), Krasicki was well aware of the function of irony in his own society. After all, the social background in Poland under King Stanislas Augustus was not greatly different from that of Swift's England or Voltaire's France (though the political and economic backgrounds were). Everywhere, enlightened people, especially writers, were forced to make a clear distinction between the rational minority (themselves) endowed with their share of reason, judgment, common sense and wit, struggling throughout the period to improve general standards of conduct and morality in society—and the ill-educated, ignorant, reactionary mob, a group corresponding in Poland to Krasicki's gentry, especially those in the rural areas. Although Krasicki's Squire is a member of the rural gentry, he is far from being typical of that group, who spent their time for the most part—as did their English counterparts—isolated on their country estates or farms, rarely visiting the capital, never buying or reading a book (unless it were a prayer-book or calendar), reeking of stables, tobacco and strong drink, and finding entertainment in coarse jests and horse-play. That this view of the Polish gentry in the provinces during the reign of King Stanislas Augustus is not unduly exaggerated is demonstrated by Kaczkowski's popular historical tale *The Battle for the Warrant Officer's Daughter* (1851), set in the Augustan age and abounding in descriptions of provincial gentry passing their time fighting, drinking themselves into a stupor and perpetrating practical jokes of a coarse and ribald nature.

This marked division of society into two strata (the peasants hardly counted) meant that writers had to bear in mind two audiences. They hoped to be able to reach the gentry as well as their enlightened contemporaries, but to achieve this feat it was necessary to adopt the two voices so characteristic of eighteenth-century writing. Krasicki's *Adventures of Nicholas Find-Out* can be read in two ways, as can *Gulliver's Travels, Rasselas* or *Candide:* on the surface, these are interesting and amusing accounts of travel and adventure (to be sure, their narrative interest today is slight, but our taste in narrative is considerably more sophisticated than was eighteenth-century taste). But Krasicki's more en-

Conclusion

lightened readers could discern the satirical and ironic meaning of the book, and enjoy it—as he intended them to—on both levels. The same principle operates throughout Krasicki's writing, and is most apparent in his fables and satires: the unenlightened reader can enjoy the story, the wit and humor, without applying the moral to himself. That Krasicki did not always succeed in conveying his double meaning to readers is evidenced in the *History*, where the narrative is too weak to bear the metaphorical burden Krasicki places on it.

Krasicki's contribution to the development of literature cannot be over-estimated. To be sure, it was largely restricted to Polish and other Slavic literatures.[4] Needless to say, this is our loss. But it is salutary to be reminded, when we admire the familiar figures of eighteenth-century poetry and prose, that there is also to be numbered among them "His Grace the Bishop of Warmia."

Notes and References

Chapter One

1. James William Johnson, *The Formation of English Neo-Classical Thought* (Princeton, N.J., 1967), p. 17.

2. Robert H. Lord, *The Second Partition of Poland* (Cambridge, Mass., 1915), pp. 25–26.

3. The calendars, popular in eighteenth-century Poland among the rural gentry, were miscellaneous collections of useful information much like the almanacs of today. See Aleksander Brückner, *Dieje kultury polskiej* (History of Polish Culture) III (Warsaw, 1939), p. 106.

4. Zofia Sinko, *"Monitor" wobec angielskiego "Spectatora,"* (The *Monitor* compared to the English *Spectator*) (Wroclaw, 1956) investigates this topic exhaustively. English summary is provided.

5. Stanislaw Kott, *The Critical Moment* (London, 1964), p. 155.

6. For a more detailed account, see David J. Welsh, *Russian Comedy 1765–1823* (The Hague, 1966).

7. Maria Renata Mayenowa, Introduction to *Ludzie Oświecenia o języku i stylu* (Age of Enlightenment on Language and Style) I (Warsaw, 1958).

Chapter Two

1. Maynard Mack, ed., *Essential Articles for the Study of Alexander Pope* (Hamden, Conn., 1964), p. 87.

2. Francis Gallaway, *Reason, Rule and Revolt in English Classicism* (New York, 1965), *passim*.

3. For a more detailed account, see David J. Welsh, *Adam Mickiewicz* (New York, 1966) *passim*.

4. Juliusz Kleiner, *O Krasickim i o Fredrze* (On Krasicki and Fredro) (Wroclaw, 1956), pp. 28–36.

5. Geoffrey Tillotson, Introduction to *The Rape of the Lock and Other Poems* (London, 1940), p. 110.

6. Leo Spitzer, *Linguistics and Literary History* (New York, 1962), p. 110.

7. Winifred Nowottny, *The Language Poets Use* (London, 1962), p. 10.

8. Eduard Norden, ed., *P. Vergilius Maro Aeneis VI*, (Leipzig-Berlin, 1916), p. 391.

9. Maurice Platnauer, *Latin Elegiac Verse* (Cambridge, 1951), p. 104.

10. Maria Dluska, *Proba teorii wiersza polskiego* (Towards a Theory of Polish Versification) (Warsaw, 1962), p. 58.

11. W. F. Jackson Knight, *Roman Vergil* (London, 1944), p. 259.

12. Geoffrey Tillotson, *On the Poetry of Pope* (Oxford, 1938), p. 144.

13. Lawrence Richardson, *Poetical Theory in Republican Rome* (New Haven, 1944), p. 23.

Chapter Three

1. Wladyslaw Smoleński, *Przewrot umyslowy w Polsce w XVII w.* (The Intellectual Revolution in Eighteenth-century Poland) (Warsaw, 1923), pp. 131ff.

2. Wojciech Podgórski, "Z okazji 'vitrum gloriosum' w *Monachomachii*," (On the 'vitrum gloriosum' in *Battle of Monks*) *Ruch literacki* (Literary Movement) VI (no. 28) (1966), pp. 21–23.

3. David J. Welsh, "At the Sign of the Poets: Gröll's Printing House in Warsaw," *Slavonic and East European Review* XLI (no. 96) (1962), pp. 213–14.

Chapter Four

1. Julian Krzyzanowski, *Historia literatury polskiej* (History of Polish Literature) (Warsaw, 1964), pp. 66ff. Indexed under "Ezop."

2. Translated by Professor W. J. Rose in *Slavonic and East European Review* XXVIII (1949), p. 5. Quoted by permission of the Editor.

3. Juliusz Kleiner, *op. cit., passim.*

4. David J. Welsh, *Adam Mickiewicz (op. cit.)*, p. 141.

5. Translated by Jerzy Peterkiewicz and Burns Singer, *Five Centuries of Polish Poetry* (London, 1960), p. 53. Quoted by kind permission of Mrs. Singer.

6. W. J. Rose (*op. cit.*), p. 6.

7. *Ibid.*, p. 6.

8. See note 5 above.

Chapter Five

1. An excellent account is given by Czeslaw Zgorzelski, "Naruszewicz—poeta" (Naruszewicz as Poet) *Rocznik humanistyczny* (Humanistic Annual) IV (1953/1955), pp. 109–42.

2. For a more detailed account, see David J. Welsh, *Russian Comedy (op. cit.)*, pp. 51–61.

Chapter Six

1. Francis Gallaway, *op. cit.*, 111–116, 320–323.
2. Julian Krzyzanowski, *Romans polski XVI w.* (The Sixteenth-century Polish Romance) (Warsaw, 1962).
3. Francis Gallaway, *op. cit.*, *passim.*

Chapter Seven

1. Zbigniew Golanski, "Metryka *Pana Podstolego*," (Genealogy of *The Squire*) *Archiwum literackie* (Literary Archive) V (1960), p. 214. "Podstoli" is an obsolete honorary title. It corresponds more or less to "Assistant Master of the Pantry." I have anglicized it for the sake of brevity.
2. *Ibid.*, p. 215.
3. Zofia Sinko, *op. cit.*
4. Francis Gallaway, *op. cit.*
5. Mieczyslaw Piszczkowski, "Nieporozumienia wokól *Pana Podsto-lego*" (Misunderstandings around *The Squire*) *Ruch Literacki* (Literary Movement) IV (no. 17) (1963), pp. 59–65.
6. Zbigniew Golański, *op. cit.*
7. David J. Welsh, "II Cortegiano polacco 1564," *Italica* XL (1963), pp. 22–27 gives a brief account of this work.
8. The references are to Book, Chapter and Section.
9. *The Cambridge History of Poland from Augustus II to Pilsudski* (Cambridge, 1951), pp. 88–176. See also Mieczyslaw Piszczkowski, "Krasicki—epik wsi polskiej," (Krasicki as Epic Poet of the Polish Countryside), *Zeszyty naukowe Uniwersytetu Jagiellońskiego* (Scientific Notes of the Jagiellonian University) 3 (no. 13) (1957), pp. 89–137. (English summary 140–143).
10. Barbara Hardy, "Food and Ceremony in *Great Expectations*," *Essays in Criticism* IV (1963), 351. See also Stanislaw Lempicki, "Glossy do *Pana Tadeusza*," (Glosses to *Pan Tadeusz*), *Pamiętnik literacki* (Literary Memorial) XXXI (1934), pp. 444–46.
11. *Historia* I, p. 2.
12. Mieczyslaw Klimowicz, Introduction to *Historia* (Warsaw, 1956), p. 33.
13. Mieczyslaw Klimowicz, *op. cit.*, p. 30.
14. M. P. Conant, *Eighteenth Century Eastern Tales* (New York, 1908) remains the standard account of this minor genre.

Chapter Eight

1. Jacques Perret, *Horace*, translated by Bertha Humez (New York, 1964), pp. 103, 111–12, 119.

2. Ignacy Krasicki, *Pisma wybrane* (Selected Writings) II (Warsaw, 1954), p. 245.

Chapter Nine

1. Jules Patouillet, "Molière et sa fortune en Russie," *Revue des études slaves* II (1922), pp. 272–302.
2. F. C. Green, *Minuet* (London, 1935), p. 152.
3. Ignacy Krasicki, *Komedie* (Comedies) (Warsaw, 1956), p. 82.

Chapter Ten

1. Samuel Johnson, *Life of Dryden.*
2. Jerzy Pietrkiewicz, "The Idyll: a Constant Companion of Polish Poets," *Slavonic and East European Review* XXXIV (1954), pp. 131–155.
3. As witness the publication of her *Letters,* edited by E. Marczewska-Standowa (Wroclaw, 1960).
4. Julian Krzyzanowski, *op. cit.,* p. 329.
5. Zygmunt Leśnodorski, "Źródla starozytne *Wojny chocimskiej* Krasickiego," (Classical Sources of Krasicki's *Chocim War*), *Pamietnik literacki* (Literary Memorial) XXVIII (1931), pp. 544, 552.
6. Boswell's *Life* III (London, 1934), p. 183.
7. Krystyna Krycińska, "Brulion a czystopis *Pieśni Osjana w* tlumaczeniu Ignacego Krasickiego," (Draft and Clean Copy of *Songs of Ossian* in Krasicki's Translation) *Poradnik językowy* (Linguistic Adviser) IV (1966), pp. 156–69.
8. Waclaw Borowy, *O poezji polskiej w wieku XVIII* (On Polish Poetry of the Eighteenth Century) (Cracow, 1948), pp. 105–9.
9. Janusz Pelc, *Jan Kochanowski w tradycjach literatury polskiej* (Jan Kochanowski in the Traditions of Polish Literature) (Warsaw, 1965), provides an exhaustive account.
10. Ignacy Krasicki, *Pisma wybrane* (Selected Works) II (Warsaw, 1954), pp. 253–55.

Chapter Eleven

1. George Sherburn, Introduction to *The Correspondence of Alexander Pope,* I (Oxford, 1956), xi.
2. John Sparrow, *Independent Essays* (London, 1963), pp. 77–87 (on Dr. Johnson's letters).
3. For a full account of this event, see *Cambridge History of Poland* II (Cambridge, 1951), pp. 100ff, 119–123, 126, 133, 137 etc.
4. *Ibid.,* p. 88.

Chapter Twelve

1. Michel Foucault, *Madness and Civilization: a History of Insanity in the Age of Reason,* translated by Richard Howard (New York, 1965) makes a number of interesting points in this respect.

2. James Sutherland, *A Preface to Eighteenth-century Poetry* (Oxford, 1950) has been a useful guide in this section.

3. Ian Watt, "The Ironic Voice," *The Listener,* April 27, 1967. Two other broadcast talks by Professor Watt on the "Augustan tradition" were published in this journal on April 6 and 13 respectively.

4. See the essays published in the *Księga referatów* (Volume of Reports) edited by Ludwik Bernacki (Lwów, 1936), containing reports delivered at the "Krasicki Congress" in 1935, e.g. Wiktor Czernobajew, "Ignacy Krasicki w literaturze rosyjskiej" (Ignacy Krasicki in Russian Literature), Marian Szyjkowski, "Ignacy Krasicki w czeskim odrodzeniu" (Ignacy Krasicki in the Czech Renaissance), etc.

Selected Bibliography

Bibliographies in Polish

ESTREICHER, KAROL. *Bibliografja polska* (Polish Bibliography) part III, vol. IX (Cracow: Polska akademia umiejętności, 1905), 220–26. This impressive work (the Polish "national" bibliography), is now being reprinted. Estreicher lists all editions of Krasicki's works known at that time.

KORBUT, GABRJEL. *Literatura polska od początków do wojny światowej* (Polish Literature from Its Beginnings to the World War) 2nd ed., vol. II (Warsaw: Kasa im. Mianowskiego, 1929), 75ff., 126, 137, 140. I regret that the relevant volumes (4–6) of the *Bibliografia literatury polskiej* (Bibliography of Polish Literature) known as "Nowy Korbut" had not yet appeared when the present study was written.

RUDNICKA, JADWIGA. *Bibliografia powieści polskiej 1601–1800* (Bibliography of the Polish Novel 1601–1800) Wroclaw: Ossolineum, 1964, 167–178. Contains full bibliographical descriptions of Krasicki's fiction, from the Eastern Tales to *Podstoli* (The Squire), and lists libraries which hold copies.

Bibliography in English

COLEMAN, MARION MOORE, *comp. Polish Literature in English Translation*, Cheshire, Conn.: Cherry Hill Books, 1963, 52–56. Mrs. Coleman's invaluable bibliography points out the lack of translations into English of Krasicki's work. She lists some 34 fables, most buried in more or less obscure journals (e.g. the *Gentleman's Magazine*, 1840).

PRIMARY SOURCES

Pisma wybrane (Selected Works). Warsaw: Państwowy instytut wydawniczy, 1954. 4 vols. As the title of this edition indicates, it contains only a "selection" of Krasicki's voluminous works. Volume I contains the *Battle of Mice*, the *Battle of Monks* and its sequel, and both sets of fables. The satires, epistles and miscellaneous poems (also *Verse and Prose*) are contained in vol. 2. The *Ad-*

ventures of Nicholas Find-Out, the first part (only) of *Podstoli* and a selection of the *Monitor* essays are in vol. 3, while the fourth contains *History, Eastern Tales,* a selection of Krasicki's letters and *A True Story* . . . (a work to which the present study did not find it necessary to refer). A fifth volume was projected by the Editor-in-Chief of this edition, the late Tadeusz Mikulski, but due to his untimely death, it has never appeared. The work was to have been a full-length study of Krasicki.

Although this edition is selected, it contains valuable critical apparatus and notes, to which I am happy to acknowledge my indebtedness.

Most of Krasicki's major works are available in present-day editions: of these, the more important are his letters (Wroclaw: Ossolineum, 1958) in two volumes; Ludwik Bernacki's celebrated edition of the satires and epistles (Lwów: Tow. dla popierania nauki polskiej, 1908), and the comedies (Warsaw: Państwowy instytut wydawniczy, 1956). For coverage of Krasicki's writings in Polish, see Julian Krzyzanowski, *Historia literatury polskiej* (History of Polish literature). Warsaw: PIW, 1964, 588–589.

For less well-known works of Krasicki, it is still necessary to consult nineteenth-century editions. For the present study, I used the Paris, "Barbezat" edition of 1830, a one-volume reprint of the ten-volume edition of Krasicki's editor Dmochowski (Warsaw, 1803–1804). The latter edition was supervised by Krasicki just before his death. Nevertheless, many problems of textual criticism still remain to be solved by literary scholars and bibliographers.

SECONDARY SOURCES IN POLISH *(selected)*

BERNACKI, LUDWIK, ed. *Księga referatów* (Zjazd naukowy im. Ignacego Krasickiego) (Volume of Reports: The Ignacy Krasicki Scholarly Congress), Lwów, 1936. This work was not available to me. A selection of the most important items is listed in Juliusz Nowak-Dluzewski in his collection of "materials" on Krasicki (Warsaw: Państwowe zaklady wydawnictw szkolnych, 1964), 254 (see below).

BOROWY, WACLAW. *O poezji polskiej w wieku XVIII* (On Polish Poetry in the XVIIIth Century). Cracow: Polska akademia umiejętności, 1948, 102–177. As befits the importance of Krasicki, Professor Borowy devotes to him by far the longest chapter in this important survey. The work was written in the dark years of 1940–1944, and was one of the last books published by the Polish Academy before it was "reorganised" and renamed by the Communist regime.

GASIOROWSKA, ZOFIA. "Wplyw Moliera na komedye Krasickiego" (Influence of Molière on Krasicki's Comedies). *Pamiętnik Literacki* (Literary Memorial) XIII (1913), 257–283. An example of the futility of searching the works of a major author for "influences."

KLEINER, JULIUSZ. *O Krasickim i o Fredrze: dziesięć rozpraw* (On Krasicki and Fredro: Ten Essays). Wroclaw: Ossolineum, 1956. The late Professor Kleiner, one of Poland's leading literary historians of the older generation, is perhaps best known for his monumental study of Adam Mickiewicz. The essays in this volume include studies of both cycles of Krasicki's satires, and Professor Kleiner is especially revealing in his essay on the fables.

——————. *Studia inedita*, edited by Jerzy Starnawski. Lublin: Tow. Naukowe Katolickiego Uniwersytetu Lubelskiego, 1964. About half the essays collected here deal illuminatingly with various aspects of Krasicki's poetry and prose, including his sermons and the *Monitor* essays.

KLIMOWICZ, MIECZYSLAW. Introduction to *Historia* by Ignacy Krasicki. Warsaw: PIW, 1956, 5–37. In addition to the informative introduction which this volume has, it is also uncommonly pleasant to read. The illustrations are well chosen.

KRYCINSKA, KRYSTYNA. "Brulion a czystopis *Pieśni Ossjana* w tlumaczeniu Ignacego Krasickiego" (Draft and Clean Copy of *Songs of Ossian* in Krasicki's Translation) *Poradnik językowy* (Linguistic Adviser) IV (1966), 159–69. This essay is quoted here as an example of textual investigation of Krasicki's works still being made.

KUBACKI, WACLAW. *"Monachomachia" przed sądem potomności* (*Battle of Monks* Judged by Posterity). Warsaw: Książka i Wiedza, 1951. An erudite study in the history of ideas, rather than of Krasicki's poem as a literary work.

MAYENOWA, MARIA RENATA, ed. *Ludzie Oświecenia o języku i stylu* (Men of the Enlightenment on Language and Style). Warsaw: PIW, 1958. For all Krasicki's interest in these matters, he only receives a couple of pages in this large compilation (three vols).

MIKULSKI, TADEUSZ. *W kręgu oświeconych* (In the Circle of Enlightened Men). Warsaw: PIW, 1960. The premature death of Professor Mikulski robbed Polish scholarship of its leading authority on Krasicki and eighteenth century literature. Here we have a range of essays displaying all Mikulski's extensive knowledge.

NOWAK-DLUZEWSKI, JULIUSZ, ed. *Ignacy Krasicki.* Warsaw: PZWS, 1964. After a workman-like introduction by the editor, we are provided with a number of more or less brief extracts from conventional literary histories (Wojciechowski, Chrzanowski) as well as from less easily accessible publications. Intended for school use.

SINKO, ZOFIA. *"Monitor" wobec angielskiego "Spectatora"* (The Moni-

tor compared to the English *Spectator*). Wroclaw: Ossolineum, 1956. Although detailed and exhaustive, this work is curiously inconclusive. There is an English summary provided (pp. 195–203).

————. *Powieść angielska a powieść polska osiemnastego wieku* (The English Novel and the Polish Novel of the Eighteenth century). Warsaw: PIW, 1961. A thorough and scholarly survey of the beginnings of the novel in Poland (to 1830). As in the previous item, an English resumé is provided (pp. 209–216).

WOJCIECHOWSKI, KONSTANTY. *Ignacy Krasicki.* 2nd ed. Lwów: Ossolineum, 1922. A standard account of Krasicki's life and works, though Wojciechowski's approach is outdated.

SECONDARY SOURCES (*in other languages*)

BAIN, R. NESBIT. *The Last King of Poland and his Contemporaries.* London: Methuen, 1909. One of the few works in English for Krasicki's period.

BOND, RICHMOND P. *English Burlesque Poetry 1700–1750.* New York: Russell & Russell, 1965. First published in 1932, Bond gives a useful introductory essay on the nature of burlesque, then lists over two hundred burlesque poems (he admits that some of them are dull).

CAMBRIDGE HISTORY OF POLAND (from Augustus II to Pilsudski). Cambridge: University Press, 1951. Edited by the eminent historian W. F. Reddaway and others, this work is likely to remain the standard history of Poland in English. It is an outstanding contribution.

CAZIN, PAUL. *Le prince-évêque de Varmie, Ignace Krasicki.* Paris: Bibliothèque polonaise, 1940. As the date of publication shows, Cazin's masterly study of Krasicki appeared when the lights of Europe had been extinguished. His verse translations are especially ingenious.

CLIFFORD, JAMES L. and LOUIS LANDA. *Pope and His Contemporaries: Essays Presented to George Sherburn.* Oxford: Clarendon Press, 1949. Sherburn is one of the present-day scholars most responsible for the change in attitude towards the eighteenth century apparent in literary taste.

CONANT, MARTHA P. *Eighteenth-Century Eastern Tales.* New York: Columbia University Press, 1908. A thorough study of this somewhat unrewarding though characteristic genre. Miss Conant deals almost exclusively with the Eastern Tale in England and France.

ELLEDGE, SCOTT, ed. *Eighteenth-Century Critical Essays.* 2 vols. Ithaca, New York: Cornell University Press, 1961. A useful collection, though devoted exclusively to English writers.

EVERSLEY, LORD GEORGE. *The Partitions of Poland.* New York: Dodd, Mead, 1915. A competent study of this highly involved topic.

FABRE, JEAN. *Stanislas-Auguste Poniatowski et l'Europe des lumières.* Paris: Institut des études slaves, 1952. The author of this imposing momument to scholarship and industry had the inestimable advantage of access to Polish archives and libraries before 1939.

FOUCAULT, MICHEL. *Madness and Civilization: the History of Insanity in the Age of Reason,* translated from the French by Richard Howard. New York: Pantheon Books, 1965. Although Foucault is not primarily dealing with literary history, his book casts a new light on much that happened in the eighteenth century.

FUSSELL, PAUL. *The Rhetorical World of Augustan Humanism.* Oxford: Clarendon Press, 1965. Here again, although Fussell deals exclusively with English writers (from Swift to Burke), his account of eighteenth-century literature can usefully cast light upon Polish literature of that age.

GALLAWAY, FRANCIS. *Reason, Rule and Revolt in English Classicism.* New York: Octagon Books, 1965. This work, though somewhat dated (it was first published in 1940) contains many valuable insights.

GREEN, F. C. *Minuet.* New York: Dutton & Co., 1935. Described by its author as a "critical survey of French and English literary ideas in the eighteenth century," this is a witty and erudite study.

HERMAN, MAXIME. *Histoire de la littérature polonaise.* Paris: Nizet, 1963. A "catalog" type literary history. Krasicki is dealt with on pp. 89–94.

JOHNSON, JAMES WILLIAM. *The Formation of English Neo-Classical Thought.* Princeton, N.J.: Princeton University Press, 1967. A contribution to the history of ideas which can be read with the Polish Age of Reason in mind.

KRIDL, MANFRED. *A Survey of Polish Literature and Culture.* The Hague: Mouton, 1956. One of the last works of this eminent Polish scholar, it remains a tribute to his great contributions to Polish literature and culture. See especially pp. 147–160.

MARCEL, SIMONE. *Histoire de la littérature polonaise.* Paris: La Colombe, 1957. Marcel's treatment is very like that of Herman. For Krasicki, see pp. 257–265.

MOUIJ, CHARLES DE., ed. *Correspondance inédite du roi Stanislas-Auguste et de Madame Geoffrin* (1764–1777) Paris: Plon, 1875. A revealing collection, but with no index.

PERRET, JACQUES. *Horace,* translated by Bertha Humez. New York: New York University Press, 1964. An excellent introduction to the poetry of Horace.

PLATNAUER, MAURICE. *Latin Elegiac Verse.* Cambridge: University

Press, 1951. A reliable introduction, albeit somewhat technical, to the poetry of Ovid, Tibullus and Propertius.

RICHARDSON, LAWRENCE. *Poetic Theory in Republican Rome.* New Haven: Yale University Press, 1944. An informative survey of narrative hexameter poems written in Latin during the first century before Christ.

SUTHERLAND, JAMES. *English Satire.* Cambridge: University Press, 1958. A witty and searching account of the typically eighteenth-century genre.

——————. *A Preface to Eighteenth-Century Poetry.* Oxford University Press, 1963. As much eighteenth-century poetry was marked by its cosmopolitanism, Professor Sutherland's book can be read with an eye on eighteenth-century poetry in Poland (after 1765).

TILLOTSON, GEOFFREY. *Augustan Poetic Diction.* London: Athlone Press, 1964. See preceding entry.

WELSH, DAVID J. " 'At the Sign of the Poets'; Gröll's Printing-house in Warsaw," *Slavonic and East European Review* XLI (no. 96) (1962), 208–216. A superficial account based on secondary sources.

✿ ✿ ✿ ✿ ✿ ✿ ✿

This "bibliography" (which is little more than a list of selected items for further readings) makes no pretensions to fullness. I am happy to acknowledge the invaluable assistance of Professor Ludwik Krzyzanowski (New York), but hasten to add that any omissions or opinions stated are entirely my own.

Index

Addison, Joseph, Oriental tales, 96; and Steele, Richard, *Tatler* and *Spectator*, 17, 82
Aesop, *Fables*, 42
Alexander the Great, 92–93
Arabian Nights, 95–96
Aristotle, 37, 93; *History of Animals*, 44; *Poetics*, 119
Augustus (Emperor Octavian), 13

Bach, Johann Sebastian, 134
Bar, Confederation of, 132
Baroque (Polish), 14, 118, 120
Biernat of Lublin, *Fables* (1522), 42
Bohomolec, Franciszek, 109
Boileau, Nicolas, 20; *Art poétique*, 32; *Le Lutrin*, 34
Burke, Edmund, 132–33

Castiglione, Baldassare, 83
Catherine II (the Great), language, 18; education, 72; theater, 108; usurers, 58
Catullus (Gaius Valerius), "golden line," 28
Chaucer, Geoffrey, 119
Cicero (Marcus Tullius), 94; letters, 126, 128
Clement, Pope, XIV (Ganganelli, Giovanni), 132

Defoe, Daniel, *Robinson Crusoe*, 71, 78
Delille, Jacques, 29
Druzbacka, Eliza, 120
Dryden, John, "golden line," 28, 30

Frederick II (the Great), 94; education, 72; Catholic Church, 131

Galland, Antoine, 95–96
Gardens, 129
Gay, John, on writing fables, 42
Genres, 22–23
Ghigiotti, Kajetan, 124, 128, 131
Gibbon, Edward, 91
Golden line, 28–29
Górnicki, Łukasz, 83
Gothic style, 129
Gresset, Jean Baptiste: *Ver-Vert*, 34–35
Gröll, Michaeł, 15–16, 22, 73

Homer, 24
Horace (Horatius Flaccus, Quintus), 13–14; eighteenth-century translations, 20; *Ars poetica*, 32; odes, 52, 54, 55; epistles, 99, 101–2; "Iter Brindisium," 123

Idyll, 120

Jesuit schools, 93, 108
Johnson, Dr. Samuel, 20, 43, 52; Oriental tales, 96; *Rasselas*, 71
Juvenal (Decimus Junius Juvenalis), 54

Karamzin, Nikolai Mikhailovich, 92
Kleiner, Juliusz, 46
Kniaźnin, Franciszek, 42
Kochanowski, Jan, 19, 123, 124
Kochanowski, Piotr, 26
Kolof, Mitzler de, 15, 73